ONE

PUBLISHED BY BRANDON PUBLISHING

BRANDON PUBLISHING LLC.,
P.O. BOX 7310
FLINT, MICHIGAN 48507
U.S.A.

BRANDON PUBLISHING DISTRIBUTION

FIRST EDITION

978-0-9886837-1-6

LAYOUT DESIGN: *BRANDON PUBLISHING CONSULTING HOUSE*

ONE

TO GOD FOR BRINGING ME INTO THE LIGHT
MY FATHER FOR INTRODUCING ME TO THE CHURCH
MY WIFE FOR BELIEVING IN ME AND SEEING THE VISION THROUGH
TO FLINT, MICHIGAN FOR LAYING THE FOUNDATION THAT HAS ALLOWED
ME TO BE ALL THAT I CAN BE
AMEN

ONE

BY KELLEN E. BRANDON

CONTENTS

"A Good man is not what he has but what he does."

—Anonymous

MORE GOD, LESS ME

Before you begin this journey with me, it's probably best that I give you an idea of where we're going. This book is a collection of entries founded upon several lessons I've learned—all of them within my first year of Christianity. For this book, the word **One** initially represented my first year in Christ; but it has a much greater significance. It's the journey of **One** heart, body, and soul—refined for righteous living. One man *(Jesus Christ)* was able to demonstrate this lifestyle. His examples of righteousness are just as affective now as they were thousands of years ago. It's a remarkable example to say the least. His lifestyle and sacrifice still vibrate throughout our world today—changing many lives for eternity. **One** man, **One** heart, **One** law, that never changes but **ALWAYS** saves.

Honestly, I can't remember all of the lessons I've learned this year, but this book contains a few principles that truly stood out. My voyage towards God began in July of 2011. I was seeking a change, needing something or someone to help me turn my life around. Thirty years prior to that date, I'd lived as the world expected me to. I strived for the things man labeled *"great."* I yearned for acceptance from a world that often rejected me. Daily, I gave every ounce of energy I had in attempts to follow the world's rules—work hard, don't make excuses, be prepared, and success will soon follow. Some of these rules rang true, but most were unfulfilled.

Slowly I became an overflow of emptiness. Life had become nothing more than existing within my own skin. My world was hollow, dark, and filled with worry—I lacked purpose for my life. There were no visions of success on the horizon. Believe me, I'm no preacher or divine saint, I am just a man. What I realize is, I relate to someone in this world. My life's mission is to find them and baptize them. There's a person out there who struggles daily just like I do. There's an individual who doesn't have it all together, and is searching for guidance—just as I did.

God uses my testimony to help others defeat the sin that can plague all of our lives. Within my time on earth, I've been molested, seen numerous incidents of domestic violence, murder, divorce, adultery, and greed. I assure you that I am not here to produce a pity party for myself. What I recognize, is, I've witnessed a lifetime of sin. We all have! There's no time for us to compare whose lives have been more *"sin-filled."* We are only given a lifetime *(a time that is uncertain)* to assist each other for positive change—severing the wires from our hearts that keep us connected to a life in hell.

The lessons I've learned within **One** have helped me halt the countdown to destruction in my life. On August 28, 2011, I was baptized into Christ. I am anxiously approaching my third year, attempting to walk like Jesus did. In my time so far, I've seen the most amazing things happen. I've learned the importance of giving and what true success is. I've battled my struggles with arrogance, gaining the understanding that humility helps me focus on God not Kellen. Progressively I've become less worried about my own desires—concentrating solely on the purpose of Christ. It's been a total 180 for me.

This walk is undoubtedly the hardest thing I've ever done in my life. Countless times I've stumbled, but every time God picks me up. The dope thing is this—God's not here to condemn us. He's not here to treat us like slaves and dish out harsh orders. For a long time I looked at God as a super power, watching my every move, waiting to send me to hell. He's nothing like that. God is real, and exceptionally transparent with us about our lives. He clearly defines how to live, how to love, and most importantly, how to love Him.

I understand that Christianity and religion in general has rubbed many of us the wrong way, forcing us to feel like turning our backs on God and the church. For a long time I was one of those people. I was tired of being judged, and feeling like I had to follow all of these *"rules"* to be accepted. Successful Christians always seemed to be comfortable, happy, and full of achievement. I was none of these. My life was very uncertain, often dim, and lacking the success and comforts of the world. I'd gotten so fed up that I actually tried to create my own rules and religion. I called it *"Just God And Me."*

As crazy as it sounds, many of us have done it. Some of us are living in our own religions right now—a doctrine where rules and interpretations often change. God tells us clearly that He'll never change *(Hebrews 13:8 NIV)*.

Truer than anything else, we do need the personal relationship with God. *"Just God And You."* Yet we also need the church, Bible, and close relationships with brothers and sisters in Christ.

Feel free to throw away all the religion, rules, and traditions created by man; just follow God's teachings. Watch how quickly life begins to improve for you. In my time as a disciple, many of my discussions about God have been fueled by bad Christian experiences. Many of us become blinded with doubt, greed, contradiction, and worry. Trust me when I say, *"God wants better for us."* The Bible is indeed a massive manuscript. It can easily be interpreted many different ways. If you truly study it, God puts it plain what He desires from us. He even sent down a perfect human example for us to follow *(Jesus)*.

Often, what's needed to get us over a hump comes packaged as a new perspective. We desire something that relates and makes sense. Almost always, putting things into practice and seeing them work can be convincing. Ultimately, we have to develop faith, and give this new perspective a try. I encourage you to unwrap this gift. Take a moment to unfasten your eyes from the world. Behold the God-given miracles that are inside of you.

Strangely, I never thought to find this relative perspective in the Bible. So I never looked. I often turned to people, or myself for answers. Those options repeatedly fell short of my expectations—allowing me to continuously wander the world blindly.

Finding God through His word, has granted me happiness and peace. Daily study has provided the clarity I desire. It's become very easy to see who God is and who God is not. By applying these lessons, I am able to recognize miracles in my life and in the lives of others. The seeds of positive world change are available to us. They're planted and awaiting us to water them with our actions.

For years I relied on *myself* to produce all of the miracles, not realizing God wants to do all the producing for me. I finally had to let go and relinquish the controls to Him. Believe me, it's very tricky to give up something you think you've controlled your whole life.

Until my baptism, I was not willing to relinquish anything to God. He had to put me face to face with Him in order to humble me. Soon after baptism, I lost my job, and all I could lean on was faith. I had no idea where my next check or meal was coming from. I was far too prideful to seek the help of friends, and I'd borrowed, begged, and stolen far too much from the world. I had to tune into God more than anything else.

In the stillness, He was able to give me vision and direction. I began to plant Godly seeds through my start-up publishing company. Speaking opportunities, staff, and supporters, began to sprout from nowhere. God continued to wipe away my worries about finances and needs.

(Matthew 6:24-34 NIV) Gratefully, I've finally found security. A peace over my soul that I've never experienced. God wants to provide this for all that

follow him.

> "**Consider it pure joy, my brothers and sisters,whenever you face trials of many kinds, because you know that the testing of your faith produces perserverance. Let perseverance finish its work so that you may be mature and complete, not lacking anything.**"
>
> —*James 1:2-4(NIV)*

Trust me, I still lack many things, but not nearly the amount I did before Christ. The trials that are now behind me, and those that lay before me, I now find joy in them. My renewed perspective allows me to fish for positive lessons within my struggles. The training and triumphs have made me more mature. I am a better husband, father, leader, and servant for God. As you read through these pages, I encourage you to allow God to open you up. Whatever you find, embrace it, and pass on your triumphs to others. That's what this book is all about. In the next chapter, I'll replay one of the darkest moments of my life. Thankfully I was able to persevere through it. It's actually what led me to seek God in the first place. So again, I encourage you, become the change God wants to see. Embody the lifestyle **MORE GOD LESS ME**.

Black Friday

1

Friday nights on the town were always destined for greatness. Yet on this particular Friday, I was celebrating life, friends, and family—a new job and an engagement to my best friend—Candid Taylor. It felt good to have money in my pockets again. Money I'd earned on my own—not an allowance from my mother, grandmother, or some girl I was dating.

I finally believed my insecurities had subsided—my inadequacy had ceased. I wasn't wealthy, yet I was sure that my *"cool crowd"* membership was reactivated.

As awesome as I felt, I still wasn't fulfilled. I was just happy to have regained respect from my peers. For many years I'd been hiding my face from them, frightened of the judgment that may have come my way. For me, it finally felt good to be *"KB"* again; something I felt I'd fallen short of for quite some time.

"KB" was my nickname. A close friend from high school had given me the title years ago. An acronym for Kellen Brandon, represented much more than the title on my birth certificate. It was my image: my popularity, material wealth, athleticism, swagger, and other things I soon found to be meaningless. It became very easy to hide my insecurities behind *KB*. It was my mask, and most favorite thing to wear, an item I never left home without.

My newfound successes made life seem promising. I was out of mommy's house, had a beautiful fiancée, and a great job working at the local newspaper. I became an involved father, and started my own publishing company. Boosh! (*Imagine explosions and fireworks as you read that*). I truly believed the deeds of *"Kellen"* was what secured such a sweet situation for me. I reminded myself daily that I was the cause to this effect. At that time, I saw no real reason to give God glory for anything that I'd accomplished. I was falsely secure, paid, and doing better than a lot of my peers. I was more arrogant than I'd ever been in my life. I accepted the idealism that, *"It was KB who'd pulled himself up by the bootstraps, got a job, and created a life."* I began believing I was a king—everyone else were mere peasants.

As the Friday grew older, I patiently sat in my kitchen blaring the latest sounds from my favorite rapper. I decided to direct my concentration toward a precise alcoholic mix. Quickly looking at my phone I realized I hadn't missed any calls. It was getting late and I began to grow worried. The plan for the night was to attend a very exclusive nightclub in the Detroit area. The journey was at least an hour and my designated driver had yet to arrive.

Suddenly, the phone rang, violently bouncing and jittering atop the kitchen counter. I answered quickly. It was my good friend Jaron—the designated driver. He would relieve me from all driving responsibilities for the night. It provided more reason to flush down a few extra drinks. Briefly he told me, *"I'm on my way,"* then hung up the phone.

Jaron lived in the apartment complex directly across the street. He was a six foot seven, 240-pound man-beast, and longtime friend. I'd known Jaron since third grade. He was currently working in Japan as a professional basketball player. His season was long, and our night was young. It was definitely time to party.

For forty-five minutes we drove down I-75, taking in tunes of *"Money, Money, Money, hoes, cars, clothes"*. I had no idea of the negative effect it had on me at the time. It was my life. It was all that I aspired for—money, women, cars, and clothes—power and respect.

The world was teaching me that acquiring these things would solidify me. This is what made me relevant, and who wanted to live poor anyway? We'd done that far too long. The world was giving back to us what we deserved—a reward for our *win at all cost* and *self above all* attitudes. We were beginning our journey towards the *American Dream* and I loved the ride.

Finally our anticipation was rewarded as we arrived at the nightclub. Parking was a habitual headache unless you were VIP *(Very Important Person)*. Yet on this night, my entire entourage was important. It was critical for all patrons outside our circle to be aware of this. Growing up in the ghettos of Flint, Michigan made for much insecurity to mask. Our current accomplishments had to stand out. We were no longer, *"ghetto Flint kids,"* and all onlookers needed to know this.

After everyone parked their cars, a symphony of horns began to play; each note slightly different from the one before it. Pushing the lock button on your car keypad served as a silent status symbol. It drew attention to the personalized vehicles in which we'd arrived.

When we'd finished circling the parking lot, we greeted each other before heading into the club.

"Five hundred dollars for the slippers!" A friend shouted as he saluted me with a handshake.

"Nice," I replied, lifting my cup in support.

"We got the VIP upstairs tonight, bottles on me," another friend yelled only a few feet away. The prospects for the night looked magical. Women were piling into the building by the minute. We were on a first-name basis with the promoters, DJs, and the club owner. The access only increased our levels of fame. It also created a courteous curiosity for those watching around us. Everything had been set out. It had never been easier to walk into stardom than on that night. We couldn't help but shine.

Approaching the club entrance was always a good feeling, especially if you knew the owner. The perks of the relationship presented a path straight to the front door. While everyone else waited hours, we only waited minutes.

As the doors continuously swung open you could hear the energy inside the club. The ground seemed to thump and the people in line moved with parallel rhythm. Occasionally a couple of intoxicated women would fall out of the doors as they opened, laughing and stumbling into one another. To us they looked silly. But for them it was another great night on the town.

Once we entered the club, we immediately felt the vigorous vibes and vanity. I could smell celebration in the air. One step in front of the other, we walked the upward winding staircase. *"Stairway to heaven"* we called it.

Arriving at the top of the stairs, I surveyed the landscape. I needed so badly to stretch my arms outward. The pose signified success. I'd made it to the top of the mountain. A friend handed me a drink and shouted, *"We made it!"* Before I could get into any trouble, my phone began vibrating harshly in my pocket. It was Candid, my fiancée at the time.

"We down here! Where you at?" she asked, with a slight attitude. I knew she would grow angry if I left her outside the club entrance any longer. Hastily but smoothly, I handed my drink to a friend.

"I gotta go get Candid. They waiting downstairs." I warned.

With the stairs beneath my feet, I proceeded on my mission, pushing and shoving past drunken patrons. While bumping my way towards the entrance, I managed to catch several drops of cocktails on my forehead.

"Yo, yo, watch it cuz!" a few people requested. They weren't happy seeing their drinks on the floor or on my face. I'd promised Candid and her good friend VIP access and I had to deliver.

When I finally arrived, there were countless people gathered at the door. Both sides were packed. Outside stood around a hundred people, all of them dying for their moment to be inside. It was difficult to see anyone, let alone Candid and her friend. I began to squint my eyes, scanning the crowd for their faces. Once I spotted them, I motioned them to follow me. They began walking towards me and past the doorman. Quickly, he raised his arm to block them.

"Where do yall think yall going?" he asked with a deep baritone voice.

"They're with me," I whispered in his ear, while putting a crisp $50 bill into his opposite hand. He looked down angrily at the bill. Then with a slight facial adjustment, he replied.

"No problem my man. Yal good to go."

He moved his arm, and granted them access toward the stairway to heaven. Candid looked flawless. It was one of our first times out since we'd made the decision to live with each other. Candid and I had a long history. She was my high school sweetheart. Although we were several years removed from high school, our friendship, and intimacy, seemed to be better than ever.

For the past eight years she had been living in Atlanta. Despite our troubled high school dating career, *(all due to my cheating ways)* we still managed to always keep in touch. Whenever we would talk, no matter what type of relationship we were in, it felt like we'd never missed a moment apart.

7

A few months before she moved back to Flint, we both realized we'd yet to find anyone that made us feel complete. Moving back was a huge sacrifice for her. She was well established in Atlanta. She had a career, great friendships, and family. Flint had only me to offer her, and before I'd landed my new job, I wasn't much of an offer at all. With all of the issues and baggage as a backdrop, she still decided to return. I was glad she did. With Candid on my arm, I knew the future would be bright for me. She was beautiful, educated, and a great friend that knew me inside and out. We were about four days into our engagement and excited about the next stages of our lives. It was a night filled with reasons to celebrate.

The nightclub was full and everyone was inside: old friends, new friends, and soon-to-be friends. When we reached the top of the stairs, we received drinks and hugs from every angle. It felt good to be surrounded by first-class company.

As hours passed, and bottles emptied, my mental confusion grew. The more I drank, the less control I had over my flesh. Things appeared much differently in my eyes than they were in reality. I needed the room to stop spinning, so I found a couch and flopped down. The couch happened to be next to a small group of women; their clothes screaming *"Lust after us!"* Suddenly I began to size up my fiancée and the other women in the nightclub. Doubtful, I started to wonder about very stupid things.

Am I making the right choice? Am I ready to settle down with just one woman? Selfish as I was, I didn't want to give up my bachelor lifestyle. I'd grown too familiar with the one-night stands and constant shuffling of different women.

About two and a half hours into my liquor, I'd grown completely delusional. My senses began to disappear one at a time. My eyes saw differently, and my emotions were all over the place. I had flashes of passion, converting into blazes of insecurity. I didn't know if I was running or walking—so I decided to stand. Standing in one spot would allow me to regain some sanity. At least that's what I kept telling myself. *"I'll just stand here and scan. People watch. Yeah, that's what I'll do."*

Unfortunately my calm stand and scan granted me a moment to notice the hefty amount of superstar athletes in the VIP. One by one they ordered cases of liquor that came to their tables accompanied by fireworks and beautiful bartenders. Everyone seemed to be having fun, but I no longer shared in their enjoyment. I began to look at my hands in disappointment as if they'd failed me. I too was supposed to be a superstar athlete. I was supposed to be the one buying the $200 bottles of alcohol.

As I looked down in shame, I noticed a glass bowl sitting on the table in front of me. It was full of car keys. I couldn't help but notice the car remotes, ranging from Mercedes and Lexus, BMW and Audi. How could I compete with these men who had become what I'd failed to become?

There was no way I could catch up to the hundreds of thousands of dollars in the room that night. Candid deserved the world and the rich man I should've been, not just some guy working at the local newspaper.

I sat in my moment of insecurity for a short time, my resentment continuing to grow. When I looked up from my shoes (*that didn't cost five hundred dollars*) my eyes became fixed on a woman. She stood tall and beautiful with curves in all the right places. What I believed to be a quick peek was actually a tongue-hanging-from-my-mouth stare. I was so intoxicated that I didn't realize the time I'd spent googly-eyed over her. Even worse, Candid witnessed every second of my disastrous behavior.

The blatant lust quickly reopened deep and haunting scars for my fiancée, reminding her of the reasons she'd broken off our relationship in high school. This is where my lack of change first started to reveal itself. My decently dressed outside layer started to shed and my nasty insides began to show.

Before I could change where I was looking, Candid put herself between the woman and me. I had no way of masking my guilt. The unlimited refills of alcohol had stolen my acting abilities for the night. While starring at me, simultaneously her face grew as red as the polish on her fingers. The only tactic I had left in my arsenal was reverse psychology. I had to convince her *(I'd already convinced myself)* it was actually her fault that I was starring at that woman, slowly undressing her with my eyes. It was her fault for not possessing a body I could lust for.

I promptly packed up my false sense of righteousness and stormed over to her. I had to confront Candid about her emotional errors. As soon as I was close enough, I'd forgotten about my original mission and decided to make excuses instead. Holding my hand up, I said,

"Baby it's not what you think. Chill out, and don't make a scene. That chick was eying me. I was only staring back at her because I couldn't believe she would stare at me like that. Especially with you standing right here. She knows I'm here with you. These girls crazy."

I was hoping my charm would put a smile on her face. It didn't. She only grew more enraged. Rapidly I reverted to my original plan remembering that this wasn't my fault anyway. It was Candid's. Before I knew it, I was yelling at the top of my lungs and forcing her into the women's bathroom. People began to surround us, pulling and tugging at me, yelling to back off of her but to no avail.

"What are you doing Kellen?!" Candid yelled over the loud music and conversations. I was beginning to wonder the same thing. What was I doing and how did we get here?

"What are YOU doing?" I swiftly responded.

"Take your hands off me," she continued furiously, ripping her arms from my grip.

"I saw you looking at that girl! You still the same old Kellen!"

11

In defense, I shouted, *"You ain't no good Candid! I see you looking at all these men and they money!"*

Candid looked at me blankly; she didn't have a clue about what I was accusing her of. The truth became clear. I was the only one lessened by our surroundings. It was me, fully defeated by my own deficiency. I was the only one that was unconfident.

Blinking back into reality I quickly realized how foolish we appeared to everyone. The room suddenly became silent and still. The music seemed to have stopped. I began to retreat with a slow backwards stroll. My eyes moved swiftly from right to left; the moment growing more awkward by the minute. I guess being dangerously intoxicated can make craziness appear normal, just like the girls I'd seen stumbling out of the club earlier.

The music started and our friends separated us. Candid headed downstairs. She had no interest in being VIP any longer. Humbled and humiliated, I closed my eyes and clenched my fist. Chasing after Candid would make me lose whatever pride I had left. I decided to retreat to the other side of the room. I had to find comfort and clear my head. I had to fortify whatever dignity I had left. A conversation with someone was all I needed.

Soon after, I decided to rest on a couch. It was white, leather, and looked very inviting. There were also several women sitting on it with a space in the middle—surely it was designated for me.

The women noticed me walking over and actually made room. As I relaxed on the soft leather couch, I raised my arms; slowly they extended behind the necks of my female guests. After everyone found comfort, they continued on in conversation.

"Girl, I aint got time fo no broke man." One young lady insisted.

"I heard that girl. What is he bringing to the table? It cost money to keep this looking nice." Another woman agreed, slowly waving her hand around her body. The conversations that surrounded me quickly became annoying. I grabbed my glass, filled it with more vodka, and headed to the balcony.

Looking over, I could feel the pulsation in the club. The neon hue of lights pounded in sync with the music. For about an hour I watched the people dancing on the ground floor. They seemed to be excited about life, or at least the night. The loud bass from the music made my head thump at every throb. I began scanning the club floor for Candid. I noticed a few men entertaining her. They were carrying on in conversation, laughing, and dancing. Hastily I convinced myself that she was not the one. Candid was no different than the rest of them— women, a gender not to be trusted.

Seemingly shortly thereafter the DJ began to yell, *"last call"*. I remained calm, intoxicated, and alone, overlooking the balcony. Hours had passed and I had yet to speak to anyone all night. I was soaked in my own drunken resentment.

As the club began to empty, I slowly came back to my senses. I'd been holding on to the same glass of vodka for over an hour. Raising the glass to my mouth, slowly I took a sip. The drink had become pure watery disgust. I swished the sour fluids around my jaws, then spat it back into the glass.

The bottom floor was beginning to clear out. Candid and her guest had disappeared. I was certain that she would not have left the club without me. After all, we'd made an agreement that she would be my ride home.

I reached into my pocket and began dialing her number. Call after call, she did not answer. I paused and thought of the possibilities. *Maybe she left with a guy? Maybe they got kicked out? What if she and the guy were headed to a hotel room?* Unexpectedly a text message came through. My hand was shaking for fear of what it would relay. It was Candid.

"I lft abt an hr ago & I'm drppng Quay off @ home."

The final results were in. She'd left me.

I felt horrible, more so because I didn't have a way home. I totally disregarded the fact that I'd embarrassed her in front of everyone. As usual, I could only think about myself. I was glad that she'd taken the time to inform me of her whereabouts. More importantly, I had to find an alternate route home.

Jaron linked up with a few friends and planned on entertaining them a bit more in Detroit. He offered for me to join but I knew it wasn't a good idea. Luckily, I found some friends who were heading my way. While walking to their truck,

I continued to mumble about how angry I was. Honestly, I was just embarrassed. I couldn't believe the nerve of Candid, leaving me in Detroit without a way home.

Once in the truck, the first 10 minutes of the ride was silent. My good friend Bert Randall was the driver. At the time, he was enjoying a successful NBA career for a team out east. Bert was legendary in the city of Flint for his athletic achievements. On the outside he had everything I wanted, a family, money, and a career in the NBA. The other passenger in the truck with us was Sara Randall, his wife. Sara was a former model turned mother. Through hearsay, I was aware that their relationship was having some problems—but I didn't have the facts. At the time they seemed to be a wealthy black couple enjoying their fame, access, and liquor.

With 99% of my concentration upon myself, I hardly noticed the negative energy between the two of them. I could no longer bear their silence and I spoke. *"Can I ask y'all something?"* I blurted out. I was totally unaware that Bert and Sara were working on a divorce. They probably weren't the best people to get relationship advice from. Quickly and convincingly I explained the situation and my stance. I was looking for my friend Bert to make me feel secure, but he said nothing. Instead, his soon-to-be ex-wife gave me 45 minutes worth of *scorned black female.* She made sure she reminded me that I was a worthless piece of trash. She also made me aware that I could not continue to act in the manner modeled earlier at the nightclub.

As we pulled into my apartment complex, Mrs. Randall concluded her speech.

"You need to go in that apartment and apologize to your woman. Let her know that you are going to be a better man from here on out!"

"Ok. I will do that. You're right," I replied.

I felt like I'd been dragged into the backyard and beaten to a pulp. My manhood had become verbally mutilated although a lot of her points that night were spot-on. I wasn't being a man at all. I was a selfish jerk only concerned about my own pleasures.

"'Ight Bert, I'll holla at you later," I finished, exiting the truck. Bert remained silent. He tilted his head downward but refused to make eye contact with me. It was the same stance *(no stance at all)* he'd taken the entire ride home. I guess he knew there was no need to fuel an already angry woman. I shut the door and began to walk toward our apartment.

My walk was clean and seemingly sober. My mind was clear and I had the perfect plan of what I would say to Candid. I knew I could make this situation right. I had everything figured out in my mind. I would first apologize, then manipulate the issue to make myself look far better than I was.

I fumbled with my keys for a few minutes, then entered the apartment. It was dark, cold, and quiet. I wondered if Candid had even come home yet. I threw my keys onto the couch and kicked my shoes off. My feet were extremely sweaty, as if I'd danced in water with my socks on. I took a few deep breaths, then headed back toward our bedroom forcefully pushing the door open. There she lay, sound asleep. I flipped the light switch on as loudly as I could.

"Wake up!" I demanded. Candid rolled over and looked faintly at me. She pulled the covers quickly over her eyes to block the light—that or my face, I'm still not sure. Gripping the covers, I pulled the bedspread as hard as I could. Shivering, cold, and angry, she began to yell curses at me. Quickly she launched a pillow at my head.

"Candid, I want to talk." I pleaded. *"I'm sorry for what happened at the club tonight."* Candid was in no mood for conversation. My heart told me to call it a night, but my pride demanded I solve our issues right away. I had just received the *men are dogs* lecture for forty-five minutes. I knew that I had to make our situation right. So I began to ramble in a commanding voice about who's actions were incorrect. I felt it important to let her know who was responsible for the embarrassments in the club. With a high level of arrogance I explained to Candid how our situation was going to resolve itself.

"We're going to forgive each other for tonight. You messed up and so did I." All of my demands had to be met right that second. I would not settle for anything less.

After a while I only heard myself talking, and talking, and talking. Mumbling words that built monuments of nothingness to Candid.

It was the same old Kellen and nothing had

changed in my heart. Candid was well aware of it, and I was fooling no one.

I continued to natter nothingness into her ears until she'd had enough. Swiftly, she sat up and began yelling disrespectful criticisms of my conduct. I couldn't handle it and lost my cool. I grew furious at her words. Before long we were both yelling at the top of our lungs. Neither of us could make out what the other was saying. Only chopped bits and pieces of our dialogue were understood.

"Kellen I F#**% hate you! You think you're God's gift to earth. You're not you f%&*** A#%^!!"

"Well Candid, you're not so great either! Always acting stank, never giving anyone a smile because you think every woman I speak to is a f%#!*$% threat to you! Why are you so d@&# insecure?"

"Insecure? Really Kellen? Who's always asking me if they are the best sex partner I've had? Who's always asking if I still keep in contact with Reggie? Who's really the insecure one Kellen? You or me?"

Nothing positive was heard that night from either of us. I began to beat on my chest shouting and demanding the respect that a man deserved. But I was not a man at all. I was an immature boy, only concerned with my own selfish desires, never fully caring for anyone but myself. That night, I displayed sizable amounts of disrespect to Candid. Before I could finish my last words, Candid had grown incensed with anger. She drew back her right hand and knocked over a lamp. As it crashed to the ground, the bulb shattered and sparked. Smoke began to seep upward from the carpet.

As the room went black and the scent of burning carpet drifted through the air, it afforded us the first seconds of silence since I'd entered the room. Candid reached over and grabbed a glass of water from atop the nightstand. Angrily, she poured everything in the glass onto the floor.

As I observed her actions I grew more enraged. I etched out everything wrong about her behavior.

"Are YOU crazy?" I screeched at the top of my lungs.

"I just might be!" She roared. Again I began to shoot piercing insults at her like an archer at war. I had no desire to leave anything positive in her soul alive. As I mustered my insolence-filled parting shot, I was awakened by an unexpected encounter. A right hook to my bottom lip. The impact of the blow sent me into a daze. Then I exploded.

Full of fury and with no respect left, I reached for her body. I grabbed her, hoping my strength would quickly make her realize her error in striking me. It was the first time I had ever been punched by a woman. I only knew one way to react.

As we rolled off of the bed and onto the floor, she continued to shout poisonous slurs at me, still attempting to strike me with her fists. Her insults drained every ounce of positivity I had left. I quickly became empty and insecure. I was convinced that Candid had no respect for me at all.

Sadly, I never thought to concern myself with the pain I knew she felt—the wounds revisited from my harsh words and actions. I'd forced her to live daily with insecurity due to my many sins against her, past and present. I was too selfish to think about anyone but Kellen. That was just the way it was. I'd been that way my entire life.

Slowly I rose up, I wanted to disconnect myself from the foolishness that was occurring—wbut I couldn't allow myself to leave in such a weak manner. I grabbed the lamp off of my dresser and flung it into the wall. It shattered and sparked as it crashed to the floor. It was an explosion far greater than the one Candid caused earlier. As I left the room, I gazed at her with a piercing eye. I wanted to make sure she was intimidated and understood who was boss.

In less than ten minutes our entire world unraveled. There was only the sound of breathing and weeping. Shrill words and impractical actions seemed to have disconnected us for good. Walking into our bedroom that night, I actually believed I was close to a sincere apology. In reality, I was a great distance from changing anything in my character. I knew it was the end.

There was no manipulation or charming lie I could dream up to retrieve us from this relational disaster. I had tossed and shattered whatever was left in our relationship. I'd flung her love and devotion for me around far too many times. Finally, her heart shattered beyond repair. Our anger, alcohol, and unresolved past led us to this fatal place: the death of our relationship.

Hours passed, Candid was gone, and I found myself blaming everyone else. I blamed the women and men who'd wronged me and made it hard for me to trust. I blamed the streets of Flint for making me hyperactive and angry. I blamed my uncles and mentors for assuring me that sleeping around was acceptable. I blamed the woman in the nightclub for dressing so inappropriately. I blamed my mother for allowing me to witness men treat her badly and never deciding to leave them. The only person I'd yet to blame was myself. I couldn't. At that time, I saw no error in my ways.

Many times in my life I enjoyed the stillness of being alone. I loved the silence, clarity, and calmness. But I'd never felt so alone in my life. The only thing left to do was end it. Take myself out of this world, that way I could no longer hurt innocent hearts again. Luckily, I was a coward. I could not orchestrate for myself a slow death. I had no access to a gun, and I couldn't imagine cutting my wrists. In the end I couldn't muster up the courage to kill myself. Thankfully, I would never entertain that plan again.

That night I shed waterfalls of tears. I prayed for guidance and truth. When things turned sour, God was usually the first person I called on. The reality of my life was simple. I was alone. No friends, clothes, or other material possessions to mask me. It was time to look Kellen in the face. Sadly, I hated everything I saw looking back at me.

Saturday

When I awoke the next morning, I looked to my left and there was no one. For the past few months every morning I would see her. But she was not there. I was left with a dead and empty feeling that I'd never experienced before. I missed Candid tremendously, and the guilt on my heart was heavier than I could carry. I reached for my phone, hoping to see that she shared the same emptiness I did. I was hoping wholeheartedly that she'd reached out to me. I was sure that after a night alone she'd realize how much we needed each other.

As I glanced down at my phone, I noticed my in-box had two new messages. Quickly, I became excited. Upon opening the new texts sadly I realized neither of them were from Candid. The demoralizing reality was that she hadn't reached out at all. I'd become disinterested with life all over again.

The two messages were reminders from my good friends Carey and Tony. Our friendships sprouted from heated basketball battles at the local rec-center. The sweat, trash-talk, and cultural chemistry of pick-up basketball grew into a tightly woven relationship with the both of them. We'd planned a dinner date months in advance, long before my heart had grown heavy from the incidents of *Black Friday*. A *Guys night* of some sort. Unfortunately for them I had no interest in doing anything that didn't involve Candid.

Hours passed as I moped around our apartment, constantly checking my phone, hoping that Candid had something to say to me. I listened to music but it wasn't the same. I reached out to my daughter hoping to have my spirit uplifted—but her angelic voice was not a cure. I was completely unable to hide the fact my soul was defeated. I tried to cook but nothing tasted right. My heart had sunken to the bottom of my feet. Every step felt like I was trampling over my heart. Sitting alone had never been so painful.

Six o'clock arrived quicker than I thought. Carey and Tony both called to make sure everything was still on schedule. I wanted to cancel but I couldn't. I picked up the phone hoping for a way out—or a cancellation on their end; either of the two would suffice.

"Tony, I don't feel like driving bro. Can you scoop me up?" I said fishing for an exit from the night's events.

"Sure man, don't worry about it. It's on the way." He replied with joy.

By the time Tony arrived at our apartment, my feelings about the outing had yet to change. I struggled to convince myself that I needed to get out, get some fresh air, and be *"single"* again.

From the moment Tony picked me up until the time we arrived at the restaurant was a blur. Actually, I don't remember much of anything from that outing. All I could think about was how much of a screw-up I was. I began to understand how selfish and un-authentic I'd become. The momentum of my *pity party* continued to grow.

Have you ever lied to yourself so much that you believe you're something you're not? When your own falsehoods become so consistent that they're converted into realities? That's exactly where I'd landed myself. Believing in my own lies, I was living as a person that could only see one thing—himself.

I'd always thought of myself as a pretty unselfish guy. I honestly believed I cared a great deal for others. I really assumed I was a good person. The people who'd decided to walk out of my life only did so because they were bad people. They were the liars, not me.

I sat through dinner with Tony and Carey in a daze, drifting in and out of conversations about women, money, and power. I realized that these things no longer drew my interest. My friends at the table knew me as a *ladies' man*. They understood my ambitions to gain material and financial success. It was attractive to them because they shared the same interests.

For some reason, on that day, God granted me a position in the light. He gave me a glimpse of a mind that had no interest in sinful things. It forced me to reflect on what was truly important in my life. Finally, I understood that I would never be satisfied. I had to make immediate changes—for the better—changes for God.

"Let's get out tonight," Carey said as I continued sitting dazed and distant. He began clapping his hands and moving his body in an un-rhythmic manner. The awful dance moves caused me to smirk. I laughed, then fell back into pity.

"What's up with you tonight, Kellen?" He asked. *"You seem dazed."*

He was right. I was. I didn't feel comfortable sharing what was racing through my mind. I simply replied, *"I'm good."*

There was a slight pause of concern, almost immediately the conversations of lust and materialism resumed. My stomach began to turn. For the first time in my life, I was not interested in a woman's butt or her breasts. I didn't care about what kind of car I had, or how quickly I could earn a million dollars. I just wanted my family back.

Shortly thereafter my phone began to ring. It was Candid. My heart skipped several beats as I answered quickly.

"Hey!" I began. I was excited to share with her

the epiphanies I'd had since she left.

"Are you home?" she asked with a drop of worry in her voice.

"Naw, I'm out with Carey and Tony."

"Oh," she replied, seemingly disappointed. *"Well, I am on my way home to get some things, and I just wanted to know if you were there?"*

I countered swiftly. *"I'm not but I will be on my way soon. Can we talk?"*

"Actually Kellen, I'd rather that we didn't."

I was floored. I feared the worst and immediately lost faith in my prayers and epiphanies from earlier.

"Yo, I gotta get home," I said, turning toward Carey in a panic.

"I'll take you," replied Tony.

Candid hung up the phone. I could see the concern on the faces of Carey and Tony. They were aware that something was terribly wrong. As good friends often do, they were okay with sacrificing our night. Their main concern was my happiness. Catching Candid at our apartment had become my number one priority.

The ride home with Tony was also a blur. He continued to talk, asking relationship questions and so on. I couldn't focus on anything he was saying. I just wanted to get home to Candid. I was completely disengaged with his topics. Noticing my nervousness, Tony finally asked, *"What's going on with you man?"*

I was hesitant to answer, but I needed to vent. I retold everything that happened the night before. It only made my heart heavier. I could tell that Tony was shocked by what he'd heard. He sunk into his seat, seemingly embarrassed. When I finished the story, his blank stare resurrected feelings of judgment and embarrassment. I felt ashamed.

How could I put my hands on her? How did we get to this point? As we pulled into the complex, we both spotted Candid walking from the apartment. She was carrying a few boxes and heading towards her car.

Softly Tony began to speak, *"Hey man, I'm not gonna hold you. I wanna get out and say hey to Candid, but it looks like I probably shouldn't."*

Candid's face was red as an apple; her eyes were filled with tears.

"Go settle this. Get your lady back. I love you guys and I know this will work out." Tony shook my hand, nodding his head with confidence.

I starred at him for a moment—my heart overflowing with shame. There was something in Tony's face that gave me hope. I tightened my grip on his hand then let go. Grabbing the door handle, I got out of the car.

While walking toward the apartment Candid and I crossed paths. She seemed to have no plans to look at me or even speak. I didn't know what to do. The only advice my heart could give me was to embrace her and so I did—squeezing her like I would never see her again. Actually, I was unsure If I ever would. She began to cry, placing her head into my chest. I was still her place of comfort and she was mine. We stood there for minutes, yet it seemed like hours. Sniffles and tears were our only forms of communication. Looking down and directly into her face, I asked her:

"Are you coming back in?"

She nodded and began walking back toward her car.

For the first time that day I felt relief. I was grateful that we would have the chance to talk and hold each other again. Or at least I thought.

Candid walked back in the house and continued to gather her things, not saying one word to me. After about twenty minutes, she'd loaded most of her needs into her car. We hadn't spoken one word to each other since our earlier embrace. I truly believed that I had no control over not losing her. This time it was for real. I couldn't handle my hopeless feelings.

Candid was now standing in the hallway between our bedroom and the exit. Now and forever, it was the beginning and end of us. It was a heart shattering feeling, that words cannot explain. Slowly, her eyes moved upward until they met with mine.

"I am going to my mom's to live. I will let you know what I figure out," she continued softly but hurt. *"I will help you pay the remainder of the rent until the lease is up."*

I was confused, and could find no response to her statement—no speech to emotionally grip her. I searched my mind for something clever or soothing to say, something that would ignite her. Yet there was nothing. She waited briefly for my reply then began to walk toward the door. I knew that I had to say something to keep her inside the apartment.

I understood that if she walked out the door, things between us would never be the same. The moment I'd been dreading the last twenty-four hours was now upon me—and again I had no plan. All I had was the honesty that rested within my heart.

"So this is it?" I shouted.

"You're just gonna leave?" My voice began to tremble as my eyes filled with tears.

"We can't quit on us! We can't throw in the towel. We both got issues. I'm messed up and so are you. But who out there is better? Who's a better teammate for me? Nobody! Nobody but you! I know some things need to be changed within me. I know. But we gotta fight for this. We just gotta."

Candid stared at me, surprised, but she had no interest in fighting. She had fought long enough.

"I've been praying, and asking God to help me Candid. You're everything to me," I said hoping to reassure her.

But she'd heard it all before. What was different about this time—a few tears and embarrassment? Was I scared of the possibilities of her informing others of our physical encounter? There was no more fuel for *our* fire inside her. My words had become commonly foreign. They didn't mean what they were supposed to mean any longer.

She shook her head in disbelief as her eyes began to water. She then turned her head away from me and headed towards the door.

"*Wait!*" I yelled at the top of my lungs.

"*I cannot lose you. You mean too much to me! You're all that I have.*"

I jumped off of the couch and approached her with my arms open. I didn't want her to fear me anymore than she already did. As I wrapped her in my arms I made a decision. I never wanted to feel this way again.

After weeks of conversation and consistent positive action, Candid began to come around more. Slowly but surely she was back in our home. Any other time in my life I would've become comfortable knowing that I'd won her over. Eventually I'd ease back into my old ways. But this time was different. I knew that Candid was the woman I wanted to start a life with. She was my best friend, intelligent, and beautiful. But most importantly she believed in me.

I was also aware that none of my "*self-help*" plans to help myself had worked to this point. I was sure that I couldn't think of any brilliant plans on my own. My behavior as a man was an embarrassment. I was only adding to the problems that plagued my life and the lives of many people that I'd grown up with. I was lacking discipline in a major way. I couldn't tame my habits and behavior. Although I was doing well for a few weeks, I knew that soon my mind would tempt me into going backwards. As cheesy as it sounds it's true, you never know a good thing until it's gone. For me, I'd put all of the gifts God was trying to give me at risk. It was time to wake up. I'm thankful that I finally did.

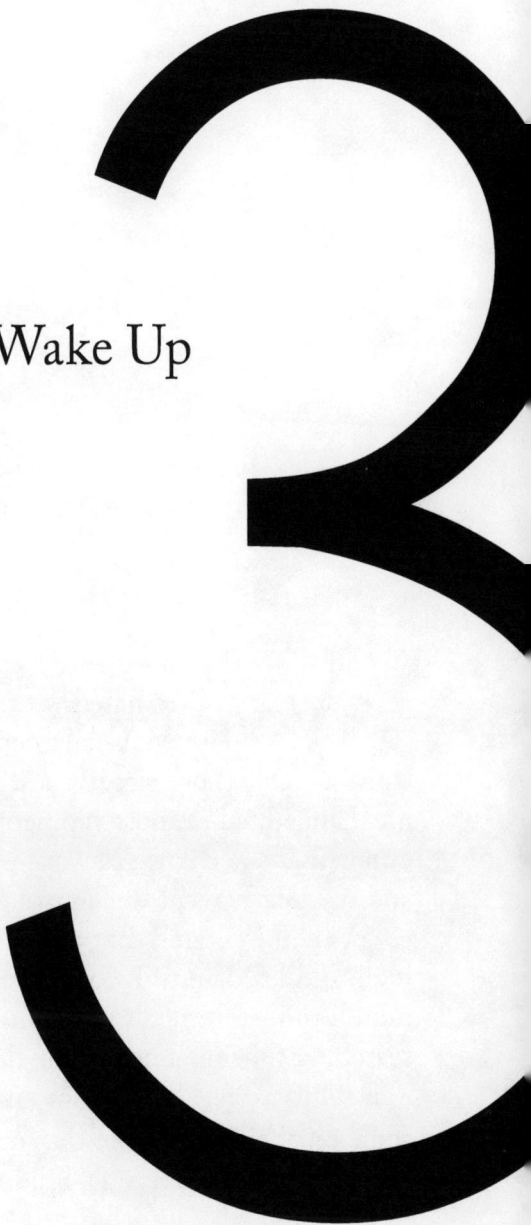

The Wake Up

3

When I glance back on the moments I've shared with you in the previous chapters, I realize how truly valuable those circumstances were to my life. Embedded in those moments of pain was an opportunity. A chance to wake up—open my eyes and see clearly what was in front of me.

When I entered that nightclub, I felt like I had it all, and I did, until I realized someone else had more. Almost immediately I shrunk into myself, searching for someone to look down upon. Why? The ability to feel better about myself had always come on the shoulders of the *less fortunate.* What it really meant, was, I didn't feel good about **MYSELF** at all. Unfortunately our world is filled with people who don't feel good about themselves. It's a key reason for the awful behavioral plagues on our planet: bullying, violence, suicide, sexual promiscuousness and the list goes on. It can be defined simply as insecurity.

Someone on this planet will always have more *"things"* than I do—but this doesn't make me of less value. It was a lie society had beaten into my skull my entire life— *"if you don't have money and material things you're nothing!"* Believing this lie almost cost me everything. What I failed to realize is that I am a beautiful creature, created by the almighty God *(and so are YOU)*.

Often the world can make us severely insecure. Before *Black Friday* and the salary from my new job, I reached a point in which I experienced high levels of insecurity. I began hiding from the world and those who loved me. I aggressively pushed myself away from everyone and everything—all due to the material possessions I lacked. I felt inadequate because I didn't live up to the story that the world had for my life. I didn't become an NBA star—so in turn I was a tall waste of talent. I hadn't acquired a professional job title—so I was a bum, feasting on the fruits of my mother's hard work. No one attended my college graduation *(because it didn't happen)*—so a dumb jock without a degree I became. I'd failed at so many things. It had to be obvious to everyone that I was a failure.

For almost two years I walked around harboring these thoughts of hopelessness. It wasn't until I felt I'd finally gotten my head above water that I actually showed my face.

"Kellen The Failure," couldn't have been further from the truth. In reality, my life could've been a lot worse. God had blessed me with so many things—I was just too selfish to see them. He had to humble me in order to reveal the astonishing gifts He'd already given me.

Every now and then we need a hard slap in the face—and I was well overdue. There's a variety of reactions that come from being slapped—shock, disbelief, and anger to name a few. Whenever I got slapped it was usually unexpected, even when I was well aware of my deserving behavior. The brunt of the blow can be hurtful, but it always grabs your attention. Being slapped not only awakens you, it humbles you. It catches you with your guard down and forces you to embody your vulnerability.

I remember each and every time I've ever been slapped. The memories stick with me because of the feelings I've just mentioned. There aren't many people who can say they've smacked Kellen Brandon, but there are a few.

Thirteen times I've had the wonderful experience of being slapped *(it's not wonderful and I don't promote slapping people at all);* eleven of those were from my mother. In her household, an arrogant, self-righteous, teenager often needed a few five-finger love taps across the face. The twelfth slap crossed my path during a drunken night on the town. I remember waking up on the ground in the parking lot of a nightclub. When I finally came to my senses, I heard someone say,

"He got knocked out!"

Confused, I asked, *"Who?"*

A young lady standing directly over me smirked then pointed at my face.

"You!" she shouted.

To say I was embarrassed is an understatement. For weeks I didn't show my face anywhere. I questioned my manhood, my friends, and my lifestyle. Nevertheless, I quickly rose above my humiliation without making any real change in my character.

After a slap, there is always a reaction. I believe the reaction is key to our growth as human beings. What we do next determines so much for the moment and the future.

Whenever someone slapped me, I believed it was well-deserved. Most times, *(because I wouldn't dare hit my mother)* I took the tap on the chin. My intentions were to always infuriate the other person; my actions played a large role in the person's inability to control their anger. In no way am I bragging, just speaking the truth. It's a lighthearted topic until it happens to you.

"If someone slaps you on one cheek, turn to them the other also. If someone takes your coat, do not withhold your shirt from them."

—Luke 6:29(NIV)

God is not saying this to be cruel. The scripture above speaks to giving those who oppose us the ultimate peace offerings. If they take our coat, we shouldn't withhold our shirts either. We should fight evil with peace—a great lesson. By putting this into common practice, we could re-define our abilities to overcome hatred. Unfortunately, many of us are taught differently. *If someone hits you first you betta hit em back*—is what I was always told. How does this solve anything? It actually creates more violence, hurt, and future trouble for all involved.

For me, though, this scripture took on a different meaning. My most memorable slap came from God Himself. It was a crushing blow that rattled me to the core. It was the result of my behavior on *Black Friday* and many years prior to that night. I had no choice but to turn the other cheek. God took my coat, and I offered my shirt as well. I gave up my jeans, undergarments, socks, and shoes. I surrendered! He had to strip me naked in order to help me—God tore the mask from my face that regularly allowed me to hide the pain and anguish of my sin.

Looking at myself naked, I didn't like what I saw. I didn't like the boy I'd yet to grow from. God showed me how terrible I was as an individual, how selfish and hopeless I'd turned out to be. It became clear that I needed help. Many times in my past I'd look to God for assistance—almost always it was a selfish request. I called on Him when I needed His power for my own benefit—never was I intending to fully serve Him.

After *Black Friday*, I wholeheartedly wanted to change. I cried, prayed, and begged for answers. As I sat alone, finally returning to my senses, God asked me for one last thing: my heart. It was the hardest part of me to give, though I'd given it so easily in my past.

My heart had been stomped on, thrown around, and broken numerous times. I'd withheld it from God my entire life—handing it over after *Black Friday* was no easier.

God was gentle, but the pain of healing quickly began. In order to get the peace my soul desired, He had to start the process of removing the filth. It was time for God to finally become *my God*—not Kellen, material things, women, sex, hip-hop, a career, or basketball. That stuff had to go! I could no longer worship anyone but Him.

When you're naked, it's hard to deny the truth about yourself. God made things clear. I couldn't handle the task of governing myself alone. I couldn't be the captain of my own ship. I consistently steered others and myself into troubled waters. My sinful behavior often acted as an anchor sinking solid relationships to the ocean floor—never to surface again. I was in a spiritual deficit that only God's divine plan could save.

No longer could I endure the burdens of *"KB."* I decided to discontinue my attempts at living up to the fake facade. I wanted the truth, because so much of my life was a lie. I was determined for change—a full body makeover. This time it wasn't about winning Candid back, or charming my way out of a situation. I'd finally grown tired of the results my worldly ways continued to give me. It was time to discover a new way—a new rulebook, where the law was righteous and unchanging.

In the days following *Black Friday*, God immediately began to remove my worries— replacing them with wonders. I quickly became astonished at the hands of God. Unmistakably I understood I had nothing more to lose other than my life. Ironically, that's exactly what God needed me to part with.

> **"For Whoever wants to save their life will lose it, but whoever loses their life for me will find it. What good will it be for someone to gain the whole world, yet forfeit their soul? Or what can anyone give in exchange for their soul?"**
>
> *—Matthew 16:25-26(NIV)*

4

Seeking The Light

I'm somewhat embarrassed that I've owned a Bible for a large percentage of my life and rarely entertained the thought of opening it. At times I felt like an atheist lacking the desire to know more about God and His word. I've come to the realization that many of us own Bibles and never look deeply into them. It's actually pretty common but not something we should be proud of.

Prior to **One**, I hardly ever read the Bible. Whenever I did decide to read, I would mainly dabble within the book of James *(which is actually a great place to start)* or Psalms *(it's filled with feel good messages)*. If I was down and needing a *"good word"* I could open there and quickly feel better about myself.

Personally, I consider myself to be a *realist*—and at the time, James, seemed to be the *"realest"* book for me. I enjoyed it because it was short, transparent, and easy to understand. The book of James gets right to the point. It deals with many topics, all of which are essential to our walk as Christians. Ironically, it became my way of justifying my own lack of obedience to Christ.

"The people here aint taming they tongue. They cuss just as much as I do." I'd say to myself.

"James clearly talks about listening and doing. These people just listen on Sunday's they don't DO IT during the week," I'd continue.

Instead of looking at my life *(and being real),* I spent most of my religious thoughts on the shortcomings of other Christians *(not so real after all I guess).* I went years without truly analyzing anything about the man in the mirror. It makes perfect sense on how I could become so blinded to my own sin and darkness.

Black Friday was the wake-up call that I needed. I wasn't happy being the dishonest, prideful, sex addict that I'd become. I wanted to love people without selfish motives. I dreamed of having a family and being a faithful husband. I yearned for real relationships—people that would be there for me no matter what. I had to figure out, *"what actions or behaviors were getting in the way of this happening for me?"*

June of 2009, I finally began seeking a real relationship with God. My voyage began with studying the Bible. I prayed day and night for God to guide me—begging Him to place me where I was supposed to be. I was clueless about my purpose in life; searching for answers the world could not give me. I was finally humble enough—or humiliated enough—to realize *my way of doing things just wasn't working.* Almost a month into my studies of God's Word, I stumbled across this verse.

> **"Ask and it will be given to you, seek and you will find; knock and the door will be opened to you. For everyone who asks receives; the one who seeks finds; and to the one who knocks, the door will be opened. "**

> *—Matthew 7:7-8(NIV)*

At the time, this scripture was somewhat familiar to me. I thought long and hard about when and where I'd heard it. Reflecting as far back as my childhood, I was able to find examples of when this passage was used. My earliest memory of this verse was presented to me by the reverend of my mother's church. He asked us to hold our wallets to the sky while he prayed for a mystery check to come to everyone's mailbox. I never got that check but maybe I wasn't seeking hard enough?

The second time, I recall an elderly woman—dancing and celebrating—jiggling her new Cadillac keys.

"God blessed me with this new car!" she shouted, quickly grabbing her walker before she lost her balance.

"For everyone who asks receives."

My most memorable moment with this scripture came seven years ago. I was having dinner with a former mentor who'd just been married a few months prior. We talked about God, faith, and personal purpose. The conversation got me interested in God a lot more. My mentor's perspective was far different than anything I'd heard previously.

As our dinner progressed, he began to flirt with the waitress assigned to our table. By the end of our dinner, he'd gotten her phone number, set a date, and gave her a kiss.

"Knock and the door shall be opened! God knows what I need," he proclaimed to me, rubbing his hands together.

I was furious. I couldn't believe what I'd witnessed. It was a moment that stained my view on religion for quite a long time. I began to lose faith in so-called *Christians* all together. It appeared that the only difference between them and me, was that they went to church and I didn't. From that point forward, I began to block out the scriptures others often quoted to me. I didn't want to hear from anyone whose lives looked exactly like my own. I could care less about the thoughts of *Christians* who weren't applying the Word to their lives. Because of this, I stopped seeking God and continued on with my worldly lifestyle.

Thankfully through **One** this scripture began to take on a totally different meaning. Yes, I am completely open to God giving me what I ask for. But it's difficult to request our needs if we really don't know what they are.

Throughout our lives we *"think"* we know what's best for us—but most times we have no clue. *Best*—often equates to what's most pleasurable for our lives at that moment. God on the other hand offers us what we need, if only we seek it.

But how do I seek something when I truly don't know what I need? Thankfully our God is awesome and always ten steps ahead of us *(actually thousands of years ahead)*.

> **"But seek first his kingdom and his righteousness, and all these things will be given to you as well."**
>
> *—Matthew 6:33*

God made it clear that it was time to seek His kingdom! So I began to pray for a church. In the past I'd been seeking my own selfish desires. I had to understand that my life required more God and less me; more desire to fulfill His mission and not my own.

Leading up to *Black Friday*, I'd been attending church pretty regularly. At that time I believed I was dedicated to making major changes. Looking back, I can't say that I was. Although my outer shell appeared to be positive, I knew deep in my soul I wasn't doing enough. Unfortunately, there wasn't much accountability from the church I was attending. It had become easy for me to lead a double life. Nightclubs, premarital sex, drunkenness, and other sinful things filled my week—but I was still praising God on Sundays and acting as if nothing in my life needed to change.

I was playing with fire—the eternal kind. Sure I was going to church regularly, reading the Bible, and doing studies. But something was missing. Before long, I was showing up to church 30 or 40 minutes late. This behavior eventually progressed into not attending church at all. I was right back where I started—buried in sin. What I'd failed to do was obey and understand the scripture completely. *"Seek first his kingdom and his righteousness,"* I sought after the church but not His law or righteousness. I continued to pray that God send me someone or something to help change my life. Almost instantly God answered both prayers.

One quiet Monday morning, I sat at work surfing the Internet and reading up on player statistics for my fantasy football league. Unexpectedly an ad for the Dallas Cowboys popped onto my computer screen. Any other day I would've simply closed the window to the advertisement, but that day I didn't. There was a deeper meaning to that sports team logo. It reminded me of memories I'd buried long ago, including the first place that I'd truly considered changing my life for God.

At the age of fourteen, I'd been sent to live in Dallas, Texas with my father. My mother had grown tired and worried over my poor grades and disrespectful behavior. I began to get involved heavily in drugs, gangs, and girls. I was headed for failure and at a fast pace. Luckily, my father and his wife were able to provide an entirely different atmosphere for me. There were many things about Dallas that changed my life, yet nothing resonated in my soul like my experiences with the *International Church of Christ.*

This church was unlike anything I'd ever seen or expected (*the building was a renovated grocery store*). There were no huge signs out front, no elegant décor or pews inside. The choir wasn't dressed in colorful uniforms—in fact there was no choir at all. When I walked in, I saw people from various cultures—hugging and calling each other *brother* and *sister*. I didn't see anyone give a handshake the entire day. My father was a member and so was his wife. I never heard them refer to themselves as Christians. They only called themselves Disciples.

I was very fortunate to have the opportunity to live in Dallas for two years with my father. The city taught me so many things but the church taught me more. Being surrounded by people who were fired up for God forced my interest to grow. I became involved in several Bible studies and learned many things about the call God has for our lives.

My entire time there, I watched people apply the teachings of Jesus to their daily practices. This was also when I was introduced to the book of James and fell in love with it. I learned about church being *"the body and not the building"*. I was exposed to the church's global strategy to pass God's Word to everyone, in every city, state, country, and continent.

I could never forget those years in Dallas although I attempted to shove them in the back of my mind. My final days there were very negative and hurtful. I'd developed a deep hatred for my father that lasted many years. When I moved back to Flint, at age fifteen, I tried to forget everything about my father. Dallas and the church were also apart of those memories.

But in my office, on the screen of my desktop was a spark. The image of the Dallas Cowboys cracked a seed that had been planted in my soul many years ago. Immediately I began searching for info on the ICOC *(International Church Of Christ)*. I was eager to find a church in Michigan that I could attend. The church locator pointed to Lansing, so that's where I went.

When I arrived at the *Lansing Area Church of Christ,* It was ironic that this church was also a storefront (*I doubt it was a coincidence*). People greeted me at the door of this small building with huge hugs and excitement. Soon after we began singing, then it all came back to me. I could feel His kingdom and His righteousness flowing throughout my body. I was home—dead smack in the center of peace. God had taken me right where I was supposed to be. God answered my prayers and fulfilled His Word. *"The one who seeks finds."* After the service God sent *the someone* I 'd prayed for.

"Enter: John Reynolds."

At the time the only thing John and I had in common was the fact that we were men *(at least that's what I thought)*. John was a logistics professor at a major university—born and raised in rural Iowa. His intelligence oozed out of every word he spoke. He was a short man with tall intentions; and was clearly on fire for God.

"Hello, I'm John," he said as he extended his hand for me to shake. *"There are a lot of John's here, so you can remember me as J.R.,"* turning red as he finished his sentence.

I could tell he was uncomfortable but he'd been kind enough to reach out to me anyway. I laughed and told John about my history with the church.

"I'm looking to study the Bible and be baptized immediately," I said.

He then followed with his signature
"Amen brother."

We nodded in agreement then embraced.

"I'll do whatever in my power to help you achieve that Kellen," he said with a smile.

John did exactly that. He began to help me immediately, pointing out what God deemed important in life. It was the beginning to a great friendship—unlike any I've had before. Several times a week we looked intently into the Bible and its teachings. The more I learned, the more I began to realize my past beliefs were pretty far from God's truths.

J.R. often called me in the morning, afternoon, and evenings to pray. He held me accountable about applying the Bible to my life. It was something I wasn't accustomed to. It made me uncomfortable at first. But after a while I understood it. He was *showing me love*, the perfect example of someone who was concerned about my salvation. John was making sure that I did not become the man that looked at himself in the mirror, then quickly forgot what he looked like. He was opening me up to God's light.

> **"Any man who listens to the word but does not do what it says is like a man who looks at his face in the mirror and, after looking at himself, goes away and immediately forgets what he looks like. But the man who looks intently into the perfect law that gives freedom, and continues to do this, not forgetting what he has heard, but doing it-he will be blessed in what he does."**
>
> **—*James 1:23-25(NIV)***

Since I was a child I struggled with the belief that simply asking for forgiveness without righteous life changes could save my soul. I'd been told many times God would wipe my slate clean as long as I asked forgiveness (*which is actually true*). It was basically saying that God was giving us the keys to commit all of the sin we want—as long as we asked for forgiveness before our last breath. From there the doors of heaven would quickly open up for all of us. All of God's great promises would be granted to even the worst of people. After looking into His light (*the Word of God*), I found that to be *untrue*. Seeking God through His Word opened my eyes to a lot of false teachings I'd taken for granted.

"The acts of the sinful nature are obvious: sexual immorality, impurity and debauchery; idolatry and witchcraft; hatred, discord, jealousy, fits of rage, selfish ambition, dissensions, factions and envy; drunkenness, orgies, and the like. I warn you, as I did before, that those who live like this will not inherit the kingdom of God."

—*Galatians 5:19-21*

Whoa, wait a minute. I was told from a pastor himself that all I had to do was pray Jesus into my heart and I was solid. My passport to Heaven was stamped! It's funny how light can remove darkness—even when we don't want it to. As God's light continued to shine through me, I began to reflect on the many contradicting teachings I'd heard countless times.

"Just follow the ten commandments!" I was told. *"Go to church regularly, you'll be fine,"* they said. I was living my life and basing my salvation on hearsay not God-say *(seek his kingdom and righteousness)*.

"God turned water into wine, you can get drunk," many stated, as they passed me two or three shot glasses full of vodka.

All my life I've heard how great heaven is going to be. How there is no pain or evil. In heaven whatever you desire will be laid before you. I'm no rocket scientist, but when I really thought about it, things didn't equal out. I didn't believe God would give up so much *(His Son)* to prepare a place such as Heaven, and still allow us to be as evil as we wanted. *"Everything will be fine as long as we request forgiveness. No life changes needed?"*

The truth is, God disagrees with that outlook totally. Earnestly seeking His truth helped me realize it. Reflecting back on the beginning stages of my journey, I realize how deep in the dark I was. The hearsay was real scripture, carved and tilted to make life comfortable—not accountable. Walking with God is never about comfort in our worldly possessions. Our only comfort comes in knowing that He is by our side.

"Enter through the narrow gate. For wide is the gate and broad is the road that leads to destruction, and many enter through it. But small is the gate and narrow the road that leads to life, and only a few find it."

—Matthew 7:13-14 (NIV)

Being a Disciple of Christ is an ever-evolving process. The light that God provides never ends as long as we continue to seek. Truthfully, the clarity within God's lessons are often hard to swallow. When I began analyzing the relationships around me, I realized that there were few in my circle truly seeking real relationships with God. Only a small number of them were actually concerned about their sin. Most of my family, friends, and associates didn't care what God thought about their lives at all. God was pulling at my heart to make a change. He wanted to introduce me to a new family that shared the same desire for Him that He was developing in me. *(Mark 3:35 NIV)*

For weeks I struggled, attempting to detach myself from my many sinful habits. I still yearned to have one foot in the world and the other in God's kingdom. With God, this could not be. He's not interested in lukewarm followers *(Revelation 3:16 NIV)*.

Attending church regularly with John encouraged me even more. The church didn't care about my color, finances, or community status, an eye-opening experience to say the least. I'd finally found God's Kingdom and His light was clearly shining through His people. I was overwhelmed with love from people that were nothing like me. We only had one thing in common—God.

I believe that life is similar to a college course. God is our professor. The Bible is our textbook. In God's class, your options are pass or fail. There is no *"getting by."* Performing God's work is extraordinary, and it should always be treated as such. There's nothing average about it. What makes it even better is that God's an awesome professor. He actually allows open book tests. Our key to success is simply to open the Book. The Book's contents provide everything needed to pass the course of life.

For my entire existence I'd been the student who skipped class *(rarely went to church)*. I'd foolishly take on tests and mid-term exams without ever reading a line of my textbook, setting myself up to fail every time. The best I could do was use secondhand information *(knowledge from people who rarely studied the text themselves)*. How can we believe there's a way to pass God's course without looking intently into the B.I.B.L.E. *(Basic Instruction Before Leaving Earth)* His Word was created as a blueprint to eternal salvation.

As silly as it sounds, many of us do it. No longer can we rely on someone other than God to save us. It's time for all of us to stop making up our own rules and ideas of how to pass a course we could never teach. We must become eager to grow closer to our Professor. Drop by His office from time to time *(go to church and pray).* He's always there to listen. Seeking the light is something we all need to do. We can't pass this class by studying in the dark.

5

Metanoia

"Repent, then, and turn to God, so that your sins may be wiped out, that times of refreshing may come."

—Acts 3:19 (NIV)

One helped me realize that my life often lacked times of refreshing. Moments of joy (*which usually came from sinful behavior*) usually transformed into worry and deceit. The fleshly pleasures of the night before were regularly overshadowed by recklessness and a lack of discipline. After so many nights of stress, letdown, and fear—I yearned for an escape from the darkness I was dwelling in.

On the edge of obscurity, there is always a door. Many of us clearly see the light seeping through the cracks of it, but never attempt to open it. We fear the light on the other side may be far too bright for us to handle. In my case, though, I no longer cared. I was open to being opened. I needed the key to that door. I was thirsty for change. Not a worldly change; *(a few weeks as a good citizen)* but a

Godly change. That type of *change* could only come through *repentance*.

For a majority of my life I had no clue of what the word meant. I figured it was an outdated Biblical term only used by characters from B.C. My good brother/pastor, Henry Shaumbert, was more than helpful at breaking down the word and its meaning for me. It was a much-needed breakdown that provided clarity for my soul.

The Greek word for *repent* is *metanoia*; *Meta* meaning change, and *Noia* meaning mindset. In order for us to make the changes we need, we have to hit the reset button for our minds. I began to work daily at ignoring all the things the world defined as *positive living*. Just being positive is not the key to God's success. I sought to see the world as Jesus did, and not through the eyes of successful men in the world. After a very short time, I began to understand how deadly my behavior had become.

Sin leads to death—it also killed God's son. It may sound harsh but it's the truth. We can't afford to take sin lightly. Before **One,** my sin was repetitive and unrepentant. My relationship with God mirrored my relationships with everyone else. They were selfish and *Kellen-focused*. I just wanted, what I wanted, when I wanted it. I didn't care who got hurt in the process. Sadly, I was never apologetic, only embarrassed *(if I'd gotten caught)*. My sorrow was worldly, the main reason my mission in life remained focused on death.

> **"Godly sorrow brings repentance that leads to salvation, but worldly sorrow brings death."**
>
> *—2 Corinthians 7:10-11 (NIV)*

Godly sorrow leads to true change. Let's think on that for a second. The scripture states, *"Godly sorrow brings repentance that leads to salvation and leaves no regret."* Godly sorrow also compels us to change the way we live. It's not designed to embarrass us. It only makes us stronger. Worldly success allows us to clean up our acts—but only for a short period of time. We await judgment and embarrassment from the world to subside, then it's right back to our old ways. When I make a mistake, I no longer hang my head for days. I ask God to forgive me, and I work diligently to make sure I never do it again. I try to focus on more God and less Kellen.

> **"If your right eye causes you to stumble, gouge it out and throw it away. It is better for you to lose one part of your body than for your whole body to be thrown into hell. And if your right hand causes you to stumble, cut it off and throw it away. It is better for you to lose one part of your body than for your whole body to go into hell."**
>
> *—Matthew 5:29-30 (NIV)*

Sounds pretty extreme right? Well it is. Hell and Heaven are pretty extreme living situations. Without **One**, there's was no way I could've looked at this scripture and taken it seriously. Gouge my eye out? Are you crazy? But what's really crazy is allowing our sin to push us into hell's fire. For example, if lust is a problem for me, then a nightclub with alcohol and half naked women is not the atmosphere I should be in. I have to remove myself from that environment totally. No exceptions. I don't go, ever. I gouged the club out of my life. It wasn't worth purposefully placing myself face to face with sin—and going to hell over. I'm not saying that being in a nightclub will send you to hell. What I'm saying is, the majority of what's promoted in a nightclub causes me to struggle. Once the struggling sets in, there's usually no one there to encourage me to think Godly thoughts. I don't find Jesus on the turntables spinning the latest jams; I don't see him on the dance floor *"gettin low;"* honestly, I don't see God anywhere. Which means I probably shouldn't be there either. As I find other things that make me struggle with sin, I have to approach them the same way. Setting boundaries to keep yourself from sin is smart. Not extreme.

Let me be clear, I didn't get to this point of understanding overnight. Before **One**, there was a huge coating of pride over my heart, and God needed to remove it. It continued to fog my vision and I couldn't see the importance of making these changes. Plus, there were tons of *"Christians"* in the nightclubs, having sex, doing drugs, and getting drunk. So why did I need to be so radical?

One allowed God to answer these questions right away. He continued to cut my soul and spirit many times *(Hebrews 4:12 NIV)*. He made it clear that there was no need to worry about the actions of others. I am responsible for my own salvation, as it says in Philippians: *"...continue to work out your salvation with fear and trembling" (Philippians 2:12 NIV)*. Only God can get me on the VIP list to heaven. Nobody else.

Before we close this chapter I have to inform you about the biggest metanoia blocker on earth. It's called **PRIDE**. A hard heart is difficult to penetrate, and my heart was no exception. Pride keeps us in a defensive mindset, never allowing us to make real changes. God had to chip away at my pride so that the Word could penetrate my heart. This process may sound elegant and easy, but trust me, it was neither. The Word is sharp and will cut you deeply. However, if you believe it is the truth, then it will begin to work immediately.

It's necessary for us to be broken by God. Personally, I don't care for anything that's broken. I'm a terrible handyman—if it's broken, don't give it to me, there's not much I can do with it. I'm so glad that God sees things far differently than I do. He loves to take on things that are broken, and all of us are. He's the ultimate Mechanic and will fix anything.

"Doing the same things over and over and expecting different results is insanity". It can also

be a lack of humility. Look at your life today. Do yearn to adjust how you live daily or are you okay with remaining the same? A lot of people are ok with remaining just the way they are. Me, I'm interested in improving every day, no matter what areas are in need. I continue to remind myself that the standard of improvement is set by God, and not the world. Getting closer to Him is improvement. Anything else is a waste of time. Change takes effort and for many of us remaining the same has become effortless.

I'm fully aware that God's way is the best way. But often I end up trying to do it *"my way."* It usually ends badly. That's when God humbles me, I repent, and we move on. Regardless of what *I* want, change is going to happen anyway. We get taller, shorter, smarter, bigger, slower, faster and older. But what about our hearts; how often do we feel the need to change them?

Hardships can make us better as long as we have the right mindset. With the wrong mindset and a lack of repentance, hardships can make us bitter. Remember, *"worldly sorrow brings death"*.

Before Christ, I wasn't getting better, I was getting bitter. I began to lack trust in others— distancing myself from many of my friends. I became a darker person, hiding my issues in the closet. I grew hateful and quick tempered. I was looking at the world through the wrong set of eyes—my own. I didn't possess the humility to realize the true source of my problems—me.

The need for change in my life was obvious. My insides needed to be gutted out. It sounds gruesome, but it's true. It reminds me of the buildings in my beautiful city of Flint, Michigan. Six or seven years ago they were old infested buildings, growing more and more rotten by the day *(kinda like me)*.

Recently, a group of investors decided to redevelop the buildings and gutted them out. They tore down walls, broke glass, stripped paint, the whole shebang. The visionary who had the blueprint all along never worried a bit. He or she knew exactly what needed to be torn down in order to restore the beauty inside those buildings. God wants to do the same with us. The world can make us rotten and infested inside. Over time we build up huge walls that separate us from God *(sin)*.

Now when I walk by the buildings in downtown Flint, I marvel at how beautiful they are. I could spend the whole day inside them. Ridding ourselves of rotten insides is a dirty job, but in order to restore beauty, it has to be done. The best thing is, God doesn't mind doing it for us. He broke me down only to rebuild me much better than I was before. That's what change is all about.

Think about the cycles that continue to infest your life. Review the behaviors that keep you and God apart. Then ask yourself, *"How can I change this?"* **Metanoia** is a great step in the righteous direction. Strive to develop a true sorrow in your heart from hurting God. We must welcome change not run from it. God's given us the textbook to pass every test there is. It's up to us to open the Book and apply it to our lives. With God as our architect there is no way we can turn out ugly.

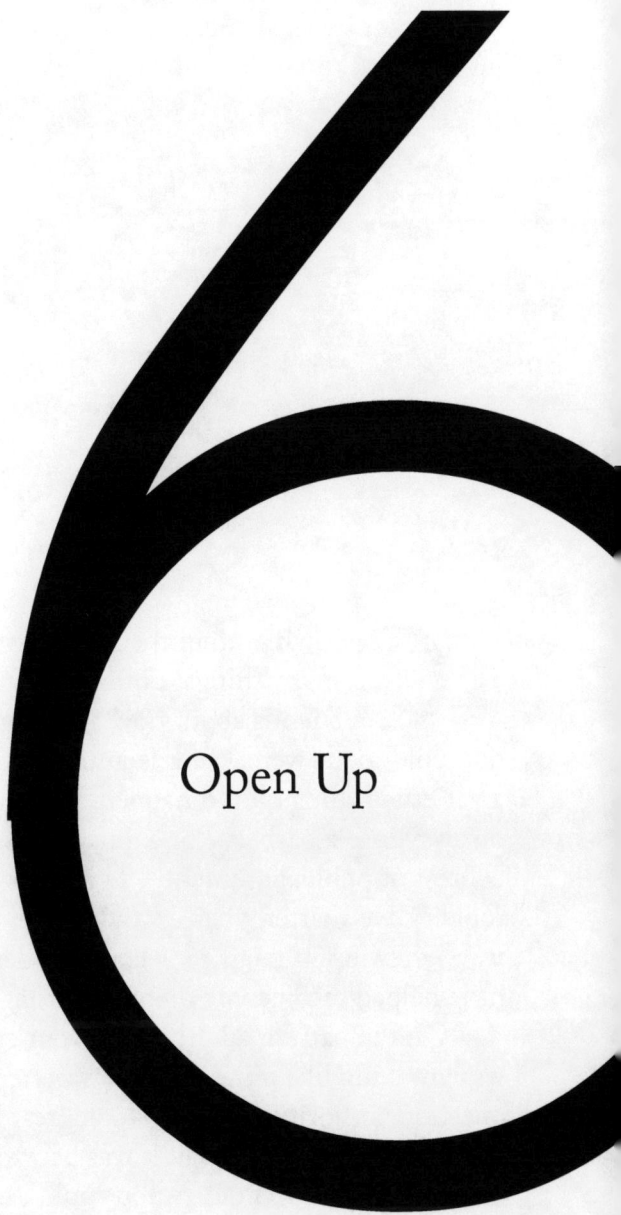

6

Open Up

Growing up in the inner city meant many things. I often reminisce with friends about how amazing and erratic our childhoods were. On a seemingly ordinary day a variety of things could happen. We could walk our way into a barbecue or a gun fight—a dancing contest or public argument—a give-a-way or a robbery. No matter what, I would never change the way I grew up. It taught me countless lessons that have helped me become mentally strong.

On the path to adulthood, if your environment was anything like mine, you knew better than to question authority. Doing so took great boldness or sheer stupidity. Either way, it was best to pick your battles wisely. If you didn't, you could easily have your lips detached from your face.

Adults in my life commonly crowded my mind with many lessons *(overcrowded if you ask me)*. I was expected to fully understand and follow them. Most were positive, and a few were negative. A lot of times they were simple sayings supplemented for deeper meaning. I often wish those adults had taken the time to sit and explain these sayings at their core. *But it is what it is.*

Many of my current life practices are based off of those supplemental sayings; repeatedly my family members would remind me that *"blood is thicker than water."* In most cases this would probably prove truthful. But what does it mean? To them, it meant sticking with your family members over everyone else. No bond should be tighter than the bond between a family.

"Family will be there for you no matter what," they scolded. *"A family is always supposed to stick together."* I could argue an entire book on why I don't believe in this, but I won't. You can't choose your biological family, nor can you make them adjust to your desires and perspectives in life. I've learned over the years that I am very different from the majority of my family members. I have different beliefs and ideas. This in no way means I don't love them, I simply cannot cling to them my entire life. Ultimately I'll end up somewhere I don't want to be. Which is counter-productive. I am thankful for my family and what I've been able to learn from them, but sticking together just for the sake of having the same bloodline is something I don't agree with. Numerous times in my life I've gotten into serious

trouble helping someone because they were family.

"Aww man we family. We posed stick together," caused me cave in every time.

God provides several examples to combat this false notion within in His word, I'll share one *(Matthew 12:46-50 NIV)*. In this story, Jesus is talking to a crowd of people. The Bible says that His mother and brothers stood outside and waited for Him. They obviously became impatient and sent someone to alert Jesus of their presence. Jesus then turns to the messenger and says *"Who is my mother, and who are my brothers?"* He points to His disciples then finishes with this, *"Here are my mother and my brothers. For whoever does the will of my Father in heaven is my brother and sister and mother."* Jesus wasn't saying He didn't love or care about them. He wanted to make the point that the will of His father is more important than all earthly relationships *(Luke 14:26 NIV)*.

My mother often warns me to drop everything I'm doing when she calls. Because she is my mother, she believes few things in my life come before her. In most cases she's right, yet when it comes to God's will, my family are those who serve with me. It's a powerful lesson I learned within **One**. I often battle with it because I'm positive my family members don't understand. But I am forever grateful for the breakdown the Bible provided me. Blood is thicker than water, as long as I'm referring to the blood of Jesus.

In our lifetime we come across many sayings such as these. They become foundations that we build our lives upon. Allow me to share a few more. *"No pain no gain,"* I disagree; I've gained many things in life without any pain at all. "

If somebody hits you, you hit em back." God disagrees *(Matthew 5:39 NIV)* and so do I. Usually hitting back leads to more violence.

"Sticks and stones may break your bones but words will never hurt you." LIE. Words hurt tremendously, often more than a stick or stone ever could.

Again, I'm sure we've all heard these at some point or another; and most of us realize the flaws within them. Yet there is still another saying that starts as supplemental then grows to destroy our lives and hearts. I am determined to help as many people as I can when it comes to refining their minds toward this mentality. To understand my first encounter with this belief , I'll have to take you back to my life as a 6th grader. Follow me as I explain.

It was a hot and sunny afternoon. A day made for incredible games and fun during recess. Unfortunately for me, I'd landed myself into trouble with my teacher. She requested that I remain in the classroom instead of heading out to play. After writing a few sentences about things that *"I will not do,"* she began to ask me questions about my home life.

"Kellen, you seem very angry and aggressive of late. Is something wrong? Something going on at home?" I was naturally an open person, so I began to tell her my feelings right away. Crying profusely,

I informed her about the spousal abuse my mother was receiving at home. I told her about the anger and short temper she'd developed toward me. My teacher then pulled up a chair and got right in my face. She held my hand comforting me. I felt at ease, then told her everything on my heart. *"I'm going to try and help you Kellen,"* she promised.

A few weeks later, I was called to my school's main office.

"Kellen, go over to the community room and have a seat. Someone will be coming over to talk to you shortly," the secretary informed.

I strolled over to the community room and found a chair. It was a wide-open area that smelled of mothballs and glue. Twitching my fingers together I waited for the mystery person patiently. Moments later the door swung open. In walks Sara Brady, a tall white woman I'd never seen before.

"Hello, my name is Sara Brady. Are you Kellen?"

"Yes I am." I replied.

She grabbed a chair and pulled it close. We talked for almost an hour. After our meeting I walked back to class. I was happy and optimistic about my home life improving.

A few days later I remember sitting at home watching television. Suddenly the phone rang, so I answered. On the other end was my mother. Sternly and quietly she scolded without waste, *"I don't know who you've been talking to or what you've told them. But you know better. I have bent over backwards for you, to make your life better and this is how you repay me? I'll deal with you when I get home. You better not leave the house. I'm very disappointed in you. You know that what goes on in our house, stays in our house."*

And there it was—one of the deadliest lessons I'd ever been taught. *"What goes on in my house stays in my house."*

Don't get me wrong, I believe my mother raised me the best way she knew how. Her scolding of me that evening stemmed from worldly sorrow; light had been shed on the darkness in her life. It was an embarrassment I'm sure.

"What goes on in this house, stays in this house," is bad advice. This quote comes in many different forms: *No snitching, keep it to yourself, quit being a tattle tale,* and several other detrimental suggestions. They encourage the belief that keeping things inside are beneficial. It's a lie we can no longer afford to believe.

"But if we walk in the light, as he is in the light, we have fellowship with one another, and the blood of Jesus, his Son, purifies us from all sin. If we claim to be without sin, we deceive ourselves and the truth is not in us. If we confess our sins, he is faithful and just and will forgive us our sins and purify us from all unrighteousness. If we claim we have not sinned, we make him out to be a liar and his word is not in us."

—1 John 1:7-10

The bottom line is, we ALL have sin. In no way am I encouraging you to confide your innermost secrets to some random person you meet on the street. The scripture says that if we walk in the light, we have fellowship with one another. I believe this to mean, we create friendships and bonds. They are thicker than water because they are bound through the blood of Jesus. His Light *(The Bible)* tells us clearly that we are not to judge, and we are to be humble. If we apply these things, then we should never come to the table as perfect. If we're walking in His Light, then we're applying His Word to our lives—so those who walk with us practice and study the same things. It makes it easier to confess, and most beneficial for all of us. Through our confessions we're able to purify one another.

> **"Therefore confess your sins to each
> other and pray for each other so that you
> may be healed. The prayer of a righteous
> person is powerful and effective."**
>
> **—James 5:16 NIV**

It is essential that we confess our sins and
OPEN UP to one another. The *saying* is clear. Pray
for each other, and pray with righteous people.
Together our prayers are powerful and effective.

As I look around our world, I cannot ignore the
implausible damage that happens when we attempt
to battle satan alone. Until **One,** I continuously
destroyed any hopes of rehabilitating myself.
"I'll fix it." I repeated in my head for years. But
nothing ever got fixed. More things became broken:
relationships, jobs, and my education, all suffered
because I allowed everything to remain *"in house."*

For years I walked around stuffing anger
towards people who had no idea I was upset with
them *(Matthew 18:15 NIV)*. I carried that anger
and lack of trust into new relationships, damaging
those bonds as well. Ultimately I was helping satan.
I created more anger and hate. Failing college
courses became regular. I was too prideful to confess
that I didn't understand the curriculum—I expected
people to believe that I knew everything.

Many relationships were destroyed due to my
trust issues. In reality, I was the one with the issues
in honesty. Frequently I kept myself distant from
those who wanted to love me. If they got *too close*,
they'd be able to take a peek into my house, and I

couldn't allow that.

Keeping sin locked inside our homes is dangerous and deadly. I think back to the mental and physical abuse I witnessed my mom endure. I still feel the effects of those episodes today. As a parent, I've run into similar situations. I remember my daughter telling someone that my wife and I had gotten into a fight. My first instinct was to *shhhsh* her. Quickly I realized not only was she telling the truth, but that I shouldn't do anything in front of my child that I wouldn't want her to tell someone else. Most importantly, I am no longer insecure and foolish enough to believe that my wife and I are the only people who have arguments.

Appreciatively I see the benefits of having righteous people in my life to confide in. They love me and hold me accountable for the sins I confess to them; they check in with me because they love me, they want to help me overcome all of my battles with sin. They're concerned about my salvation. Righteousness develops enormous amounts of purity. It helps us open up so that God can clean us out. Besides, who wants to keep years of dirt and filth inside? Nobody does, we just need committed followers of Christ in our lives to confide in. If we're following the word, God will give us more than enough family where blood is thicker than water. We'll have an immeasurable amount of people to open up to, leading us to the ultimate purification.

Change of Tune

"Finally brothers and sisters, whatever is true, whatever is noble, whatever is right, whatever is pure, whatever is lovely, whatever is admirable—if anything is excellent or praiseworthy—think about such things."

—*Philippians 4:8 NIV*

Whaen looking up the definition of *tune* I found two things. The word can be used as a noun and a verb. The noun usage of the word defines *tune* as a melody or a song. The verb usage describes *tune* as an adjustment to the frequency of a required signal. Both are key. The second explanation of *tune* seems very interesting to me. Let me tell you why.

As I got deeper into **One**, I came face to face with the word *tune*. I realized it played an enormous role in my walk with God. When it comes to following God and being an example of His kingdom, often my actions speak louder than my words. More importantly, what I *tune* into influences both. They go hand in hand. My words and actions are very important in the path to salvation. God is clearly sending a required signal. The question is—Am I tuned into it?

A universal need when it comes to signals, is to have a clear one. There's nothing worse than listening to your favorite song and the radio station begins to fade. You start to turn the dial in attempts to regain clarity, but suddenly you hear other stations blaring over your favorite song. Most times we give up on the experience all together and shut off the radio.

Tuning into God is the same way; the things God warns us against, usually cause the static and distractions that interrupt the best tune in the world. God's tune is clear, direct, and required—it's the message containing information on how to get to Heaven. Most of us would say, we'd never want to miss out on that signal, but many of us are. For example, here's a clear message from God I found in Galatians.

> **"The acts of the flesh are obvious: sexual immorality, impurity, and debauchery; idolatry and witchcraft; hatred, discord, jealousy, fits of rage, selfish ambition, dissensions, factions and envy; drunkeness, orgies, and the like. I warn you, as I did before, that those who live like this will not inherit the kingdom of God. But the fruit of the Spirit is love, joy, peace, forbearance, kindness, goodness, faithfulness, gentleness, and self-control. Against such things there is no law."**

> **—Galations 5:19-26 (NIV)**

Wow, pretty clear right? It frightens me that had I never made the decision to focus on God wholeheartedly, I would have totally missed this clear and required signal. The sins previously listed were the exact actions blaring over God's message to me. It was causing me to overlook God's requirements on salvation, an eternal party I surely don't want to miss.

People often say music and media don't affect us. Bologna! Let me ask you a few questions: Why is it that companies spend millions of dollars on advertisement through television and radio? If they knew that their efforts would have no influence, why would they invest so much? Successful businesses are successful for a reason. They understand the power of a clear signal. The world has a signal too, and often it gets in the way of God's message. It's forced me to ask myself before I tune in, *is this getting me closer to God or further away?* Answering this question with humility allows me to make good decisions on my mental food intake. Do I always eat a healthy diet? No, I don't. But I'm constantly working to remove sinful mind food from my daily practices.

When I look intently at what I'm tuning into daily, I have to realize what the signals are saying to me. When I turn on my television or radio, what is the message? Is it filled with sexual immorality, impurity, fits of rage, envy, drunkenness, orgies, and idolatry? Is it making me think about God, or something far from him?

In *1 Corinthians 10:23(NIV)*, it says not everything is beneficial and not everything is constructive. Just because it's on television or radio doesn't mean its okay with God. The question I'd like to ask you is this, *What's your tune?* Take a day and record your mental intake. Write down what you listen to, participate in, watch, or read. Then take those findings and compare them to how much time you spent getting closer to God. Once you do that, you'll be able to decide if a *change of tune* is truly needed in your life like it was in mine.

8

The God Bond

S pending consistent alone time with God has transformed me in many ways. It's provided a positive portal to Him. Growing up, I remember adults preaching about having a relationship with God, but I never knew how to achieve it. There were always the demands of, *"Pray over that food before you eat it boy,"* and *"say your prayers before you go to sleep"*, but they hardly ever encouraged an intimate relationship. As a child of God, in year **One**, I've realized the incredible benefits of spending quality time with Him.

Looking around our world, I see clearly the need for God in our lives. I see the selfishness, greed, and sexual immorality God warns us against. It's sad for us adults, but detrimental for our youth.

Sin is pushed into their minds and bodies most of the day. The first place they should feel safe is in our homes and communities.

I have a burning passion to set an example for my children, as well as others I come in contact with. I want to help them achieve incredible relationships with God any way that I can.

The development of a relationship with God is awesome. The great thing is, we're all children of God, and no matter what our ages, God yearns for a relationship with us. It's an astonishing journey full of valleys and peaks.

When I think of my days in the world, before I was saved, and what the word *relationship* meant to me, it was very apparent that I lacked a **God Bond**. I never had a burning desire to hang out with God. I thought I was too cool. Seldom did I hear Him in my car *(I rarely allowed him to speak through my stereo)*. He wasn't anywhere near my apartment *(no Bibles, no sermon notes, no devotional materials were ever in reach)*. Rarely did I find myself at His house *(church). The visiting hours were too early. Plus, I needed to recover from Saturday night's hangover.*

Thankfully God loved me anyway. But our relationship was pretty one-sided. I didn't love Him back. My lack of love showed stridently through my daily living practices. Many have argued that not making time for God didn't mean I didn't love Him, but for me, making the effort to spend time with God consistently is a must-do.

Slacking in the department of *"God time"* soon shows up in every facet of my life. I begin to rely on myself more than God. The results of this behavior can look pretty awful. Sin slowly finds its way in before I'm even aware of what's hit me. I become impatient, selfish, and unloving. I begin to fall into my sinful desires at a very fast rate. My spiritual gas tank quickly finds itself on empty.

Before I was saved, I admired and enjoyed what God could do for me, but I hardly ever did anything for Him. Imagine involving yourself in a relationship with a person who only tells you they love you after you hand them a gift. Imagine them consistently calling and begging you to get them out of a jam. How would you react?

"Hey bro, can I talk to you for a sec?" They'd ask.

" I just want to tell ya first off, I'm so thankful to have you as a friend. You're always there for me man. I appreciate that. I know you've asked me to stop being so selfish and behaving so recklessly. I'll try and get it together one day, really. But today, I landed myself into a little situation. A hard spot. I'm in trouble and you're the only person who can help. You gotta help me! I love you so much man. I really do. I promise I'll never do it again."

Once they're out of the jam, it's a long time before you hear their voice again. Do you have any friends like that? Or even worse, are you that friend? They're most certain to call you the next time they're in need. Sooner than later you'll probably cut that friend out of your life. God doesn't cut us off. He'll meet us right where we are when we've decided to seek Him.

In my relationship with God, I'm *always* the person who doesn't give enough. I'm the selfish and unappreciative friend. I am so grateful that God does *not* treat me the way I treat Him. When we truly love someone, we don't allow our relationships to be so one-sided. If we really love God, we need to make a true effort to please Him daily, not just when we feel like it, or when we need Him to get us out of a bind.

In **One**, I tried more earnestly to harness myself to God. It's become a connection I never want to let go of. I can't afford to look back, although often I'm tempted. Relationships in the world can seem so glamorous and worth it. It's easy to be blinded by the shiny things; it impairs our ability to see the evil behind them. Often, I reflect on the time God has given me on earth. It's imperative to understand how much He has done for me, and the numerous times He's made something from nothing in my life.

Our relationship is a daily sensation. I have a rapport with *the Creator* of everything. It's the most beneficial relationship I could have, and trust me, I've had many relationships. Think about it—we have the chance to converse with the Creator of atoms, the human body, and universe. Who or what is more incredible than that? Who can offer us a more beneficial relationship? Who can offer us eternity? The answer is—no one.

In just one year this relationship has provided me plentifully with gifts, knowledge, and perspective. It has also presented punishment when I disobey, rebuking me through the Word and my Christian brothers and sisters.

If you feel like you don't have a strong relationship with God, and you're seeking to have one, hit your knees right now. Ask God to give you whatever is needed to get closer to Him. Believe what you ask for; He will give it to you in His timing.

In the meantime try reading in the New Testament. Take a voyage with Jesus and see the incredible man He is. Read His struggles and triumphs. Pay close attention to His actions and how He handled others. Be sure to notice His dedication to His Father.

I can't help it, I love following Jesus in the Bible. The hearts of men have never changed. Jesus faced the same issues of the heart that we face today. He leaves no excuses for sinful behavior against others. In a world filled with evil, consistently building with God is critical. Reading the Word and praying deeply readies us for the day ahead. It helps our confidence tremendously. It allows us to step into the world clean and conscious of evil that could *"dirty us up"*.

God understands our imperfections. It's important that we understand them as well. By doing so, we can get assistance in overcoming these imperfections by repenting from them. Knowing our defects does not give us an excuse to sin. It should motivate us to strive for better. It should inspire us to act after the heart of Jesus.

Whenever I pose this option to friends, someone often says, *"Well Jesus is perfect, I could never be him."* This is very true. Yet most of us still strive for the perfect business, the perfect career, the perfect spouse, and the perfect children. We all know somewhere in our minds that this is impossible. Imperfect people cannot produce perfection. Frequently we have the audacity to get upset in discovering that nothing is perfect. It's a letdown for sure. But should it be?

Through His Word, God gives us countless examples of man's imperfections. He also gives us the tools to clean off the dirt this world will place on us. His Word is the soap, water, and shampoo we need to stay fresh. Feel free to shower in God several times a day. You'll love how you feel!

9

Got Armor?

Do I talk to God daily? Actually I don't. Many times I've carried on through life thinking *"I don't need God today."* Some days I don't think about Him at all. It's severely foolish on my part. This type of prideful behavior opens the door for satan and allows him to take over things in my life. One very important thing to know as Christians is this: the war is never over. *"sin is crouching at your door; it desires to have you, but you must master it."(Genesis 4:7 NIV).*

I often attempt to run on my own spiritual fuel. This usually happens when my life appears comfortable. The truth is, a life for God is never comfortable. It's secure, if we're faithful, but not comfortable. If I'm living life comfortably I'm already headed for doom. Have you had times in your life when everything feels good? Your job is going great, no arguments with your spouse, you have cash to go out and entertain yourself? This is the perfect space for an ambush. If you're really close to God during these times of *comfort,* here is some advice: *get closer*!

It's moments such as these that allow us to feel it's okay to take a break from God. It's the perfect time for satan to throw a wrench in our seemingly perfect lives. I call it *"The Sneak Attack".*

Think about any action movie when two or more groups are battling each other. There's always a group that attempts to attack when their opponents get comfortable and has taken down their guard. I've seen it often in boxing matches. A fighter is winning the entire bout. He's following everything he was taught by his trainers. He's ducking, he's moving, and he's striking from all angles. He's studied his opponent well. He doesn't seem the least bit fatigued and feels like he could fight for days. The score card has him winning 11 of 11 rounds with only one round left to go. He begins to think, *"I've got this thing in the bag."* His coaches, sitting in his corner, instruct him on how to win the final round.

Unfortunately, he's not listening. He's thinking about the purse amount for his victory. He begins to dream about his plans for the future. He's lost all focus for the round ahead. As the bell sounds, both fighters ease their way to the center of the ring. You can hear their coaches shouting out tactics toward victory.

"Jab and move," they scream to the fighter in the lead. *"Stay focused and find a weak spot,"* others call to the losing opponent.

The fighter in the lead suddenly decides to do things his way. He thinks to himself, *I've followed the game plan for 11 rounds. Let me get some glory for myself.* In an instant he's dancing, posing, and playing around with his opponent, taunting him with the misconception that he's already won.

Unexpectedly, the leading fighter trips on his shoelace, falling right into the left hook of his opponent. With nothing to guard his face, the punch sends him several feet into the air. Once his entire body collides with the canvas, he becomes befuddled. He's unaware of what is going on, where he is, or why he's there. Before he can regain consciousness, the fight is over. He's lost.

The truth about satan is, he desires no victories for God. Not one. He"ll *hang in there* until the final bell sounds, watching us dance around and taunt him. Comfortable lives allow us to put our guard down. We walk onto a battlefield with no armor—leaving ourselves defenseless against an enemy who is brave enough to challenge God. We become powerless against satan's ambush and put ourselves into very deadly situations.

When things are going good with God, it's an ideal time to get closer. There is so much knowledge to give and receive from His Word. We can never be comfortable in our relationship with the Creator. Until we are with Him in Heaven, desire to be nearer.

The Armor of God

Finally, be strong in the Lord and in his mighty power. Put on the full armor of God, so that you can take your stand against the devil's schemes. For our struggle is not against flesh and blood, but against the rulers, against the authorities, against the powers of this dark world and against the spiritual forces of evil in the heavenly realms. Therefore put on the full armor of God, so that when the day of evil comes, you may be able to stand your ground, and after you have done everything, to stand. Stand firm then, with the belt of truth buckled around your waist, with the breastplate of righteousness in place, and with your feet fitted with the readiness that comes from the gospel of peace. In addition to all this, take up the shield of faith, with which you can extinguish all the flaming arrows of the evil one. Take the helmet of salvation and the sword of the Spirit, which is the word of God. And pray in the Spirit on all occasions with all kinds of prayers and requests. With this in mind, be alert and always keep on praying for all the Lord's people.

—Ephesians 6:10-18 (NIV)

When beginning my walk in Christianity, I set many goals. One was to strive for an hour a day with God. Although it was helpful, I quickly understood I needed to do more. There are so many ways to be with God.

Prayer is key. When I first began to pray, I compared my prayers to those of other brothers. They had so much to say, it was amazing and sometimes intimidating. Soon I learned they had no special powers or Bible degrees from a major Christian university. It was simply habit. These men were talking to God several times throughout their day. They prayed when they woke up, on the way to work, at work, leaving work, even in their driveways before going into their homes. They understood the importance of prayer and talking to God all day long. There's tremendous significance and success in building mental armor.

When at war, it's usually a good idea to have an army. **One** educated me on the advantages of being surrounded with other solid Christians. It's impossible to fight a war against satan alone. Numerous times I've tried. Every time, I've failed. When we're in the world, we're frequently outnumbered by evil. My prideful heart *(sinful heart)* helps me believe I can fight alone. It's a mission focused on failure before it begins. I desperately need brothers and sisters around me, those who are passionate about carrying out God's will and applying His Word to their lives. I call them my *"spiritual clique"*. They've become my entourage for God.

My spiritual clique is always available; continuously willing to pick me up when I have fallen. I remember a moment this year when Candid and I had a huge disagreement. It had escalated to the point in which we could not coexist within our own home. At 10 p.m. on a Saturday night. We reached out to John and Marie Reynolds, members of our spiritual clique. Their first concern was how serious it had become? If it was a small fire, they figured we'd put it out in the morning. Yet this was no small fire.

John informed me that they were currently finishing up a dinner date with another couple at their home. Immediately I thought to get with them another time. John quickly told me, *"No way. We have to help you guys right now. Let me make sure it's okay with our guest."*

Within minutes, John was back on the phone, eager for us to come over. John and Marie's guests were also Disciples of Christ. They too understood the benefits of being surrounded. Both couples were after the heart of Jesus, often looking to sharpen each other with each encounter.

When we arrived, we felt weird. We didn't know the Reynold's guests personally. We weren't too secure with airing out our dirty laundry in front of them. It was silly of us to doubt God's people, but we were fresh into the kingdom and viewing life from a worldly perspective. Fortunately, it didn't matter. Before I knew it, they'd introduced themselves and began airing out their issues in order to help us. It was amazing. It felt good not to be judged. They too understood it's normal to have marital disagreements. The only goal was to grow closer to God.

We read scriptures, prayed, and discussed ways to humbly handle ourselves. We were able to heighten our awareness for things that trigger arguments. Not only did we solve our issue that night, we'd gained two new relationships in Christ.

I am so grateful for the relationships I have with my brothers and sisters in Christ. They hold me accountable when I am in sin, cleansing me with scripture and not their personal opinions. They love me like God loves the church: patient, gentle, and slow to anger. They are not perfect, but motivated by the heart of Jesus. They are a huge piece of my armor.

If you don't have this, pray for God to bring these relationships into your life. In the back of this book I have given my contact information. Reach out—wherever you are in the world and together we will find solid brothers and sisters to bring into your life. It's that important!

Another important piece of our armor is the Word. Consistent reading and study helps me avoid being Biblically stunted. It's significant to grow my knowledge of God's Word. I'm not at a level where I can quote scripture but I do realize right from wrong. When a friend is having an issue, I can refer back to what I've read and give Godly advice. I can also call on my spiritual clique for scriptures. They lend their knowledge with no fees involved.

A deep understanding of the Word keeps me aware in times when it's potentially taken out of context. Habitually people give us advice that is not from God. I remember when spiritual mentors would tell me, *"You're a man. You're gonna look at women and how good they look. It's natural."*

If I never studied my Bible, I would've taken that advice and run with it—placing my salvation on the words of someone other than God. Within year **One** I stumbled across this:

> **"You have heard that it was said, 'You shall not commit adultery.'[a] But I tell you that anyone who looks at a woman lustfully has already committed adultery with her in his heart."**

> **—Matthew 5:27-28(NIV)**

Ouch! This is the perfect example of why it's important to know your Bible. It's a tool in the battles against false prophets. Jesus warned, *"Watch out for false prophets. They come to you in sheep's clothing, but inwardly they are ferocious wolves."* *(Matthew 7:15 NIV)*.

I now understand that my salvation is between God and me—not my wife, my pastor, or my children. I am responsible for my own behavior. All of us are. Attempt to read your B.I.B.L.E. *(Basic Instruction Before Leaving Earth)* as much as you can. If you agree that it's the blueprint for your life, there's no way to justify partially obeying it. The

Bible is a sword helping us to fight off evil. Within it, you will continue to find weapons you never knew you had. Only through God can we fight the war effectively.

10

The Truth About Porn

Here's a fact about porn: pornography is a multi-million dollar business, which clearly translates the fact that our world is heavily invested in the sinful, deceitful, and detrimental power of porn. Porn doesn't just affect its consumers—it creeps into the lives of everyone surrounding the person who is invested—children, husbands, wives, mothers, brothers, cousins, co-workers, and so on.

I was first introduced to porn in the basement of my grandmother's home when I was ten years old. My plan was to watch a movie on a VHS *(If you don't know what a VHS is Google it)*.

As I lifted up the tape, I noticed a label with the word *Raw* written across the center. At that moment I was completely confident that I was about to watch Eddie Murphy's stand-up comedy performance. Unknowingly I was mistaken. Either way, it was a program I should not have had access to.

Using both hands, I slowly pushed the tape into the VCR slot. Suddenly the screen became fuzzy with black and cream images. A half second later the word tracking appeared in the upper right hand corner of the screen. The black and white distorted screen shifted to solid blue. It began blinking back and forth between static and what seemed to be moving bodies. As the screen continued to blink, the images became clearer. This video was not stand up comedy. It was a porno film.

I quickly realized the bodies were naked. I witnessed parts of a woman's anatomy I'd never seen before. My eyes grew larger than the screen and I watched for hours—rewinding scene after scene. Slowly my innocence and purity faded. I still remember the moment more clearer than I'd like to. It had an awful effect on me.

From that point forward I was curious about women, their bodies, and sex. I became an inquisitive little boy probing for all of the wrong things. Long before my teenage years, I was getting into trouble at school and in the neighborhood. The reports to my family were all consistent; *"Kellen touched her in an inappropriate way."* At that time, I wanted to recreate what I'd seen in my grandma's basement. I wanted the girls around me to do the same.

I never understood how dangerous and misleading pornography and our flesh can be. I guess it's because I'd never been forced to find the source for my promiscuous behavior.

When I reflect on my years as a young adult, I don't recall pornography being that big of an issue for me, probably because I was S.S.S. *(Single and Seriously Sexin)*. I didn't need to sneak around with videotapes much.

By the age of 25 I'd possibly had sex with over 100 women. At that time it was something to brag about with the fellas. I had no idea that I was feeding an addiction within my flesh—a beastly hunger that could physically destroy me forever. Sexual immorality had become my physical and chemical high.

For years I foolishly believed that porn helped me stay faithful to whomever I was dating. I would tell myself things like, *"I'm not doing it for real. This keeps me in the house and out of someone else's bed. Once I'm done watching it, the thrill of acting on impulse with another woman is gone."* I could not have been more wrong.

Here's another fact about porn: Porn is idolatry. It causes many of us to surrender our minds and bodies for countless hours on countless occasions to its evil powers. I understand that many people hold porn as their master, even though they'd never admit it. I too was once a slave to it, sneaking around my home, looking to find a quiet spot to please myself. I tricked my mind and body daily, believing that porn was actually beneficial for me. I was convinced I was killing my sexual urges through porn. How silly—that's like saying, *"I'll hang out at the crack house in order to stop my addiction to crack."*

The fact is—there's an abundance of sin in porn. Confusingly convincing ourselves that porn is a way to keep us faithful in our relationships is sheer stupidity. In no way can porn keep us from fighting off the desires of premarital sex.

Porn penetrates our minds and quickly creates a drive to seek the pleasure we see on the screen. Before I knew it, I was in nightclubs, bars, grocery stores, and neighborhood parks, hunting for women with body types similar to what I'd seen on screen. The porn didn't take my arousal away, it heightened it; porn was now my crack cocaine. It raped my mind repeatedly.

When watching porn we are actually fantasizing about another person. You are afforded the option of choosing what type of woman or man you want to be with. Remember, anyone who looks at a woman/man lustfully has already committed adultery with them in their heart. Pornography is cheating, erasing the potential pleasures of intimacy within your marriage.

Before porn, my sexual expectations were non-existent. After porn, it became much more difficult for me to achieve a sexual high—my appetite for sex continued to heighten. These symptoms sound identical to any other addiction—because that's exactly what it becomes. At any hour of the day sexual thoughts would pop into my mind.

I couldn't fight them and so I acted on them. Early in my sexual experiences I was somewhat selective with my partners. By the time I was 22, I just wanted sex however and from whomever I could get it. I risked work relationships, classmates, and good friends all because of sexual impulses.

My first year in Christ taught me that God didn't create sex for *"highs"* and *"lows"*. He developed it to be one of the many pleasures of holy matrimony. He meant for it to be healthy without fears of STDs, pregnancies, or shame. He didn't give us sex so that we could become prostitutes to people who truly don't care about us or themselves. The only thing porn did in my world was destroy it.

Premarital sex is just another form of porn. How many babies are born from it? How many marriages arc shattered? How many broken homes are created?

Porn *(lusting for women)* was and still is a serious struggle in my life. Addiction is something I don't believe we ever conquer. It's constant work, day after day. We must be aware and open to what our struggles are while avoiding the triggers of our weaknesses. I am so blessed to have God help me daily with this struggle. Like any other sin in our lives, we must pray during our moments of strength and our moments of weakness. Battling porn and sex behind my own closed doors was one thing; bringing this battle into my marriage was another.

Porn began to strip my marriage of its sexual foundations. It began to turn me away from the person I was one with. Many nights I would please myself with pornography, distancing myself further and further away from my wife. I built the belief that my wife was no longer attractive. She became a *"turn off"* far different from the women sinning on my computer screen.

My wife was designed to be much more to me than an object of sexual pleasure. Hastily, porn helped me forget that. My sinful actions flooded my wife's mind with insecurity—damaging her self-perspective. She began to question herself and her value to her husband. Porn was destructively demolishing the both of us. The bottom line is, lust births more lust. Porn steals from us the honor and intimacy of the marriage bed. It piles tons of baggage and insecurity onto our shoulders. Porn is a liar. Don't give it a chance.

> **"Therefore God gave them over in the sinful desires of their hearts to sexual impurity for degrading of their bodies with one another"**
>
> *—Romans 1:24 (NIV*

Another fact about porn: Porn is not just on film and the Internet. It's premarital sex—happening in households, hotel rooms, high schools, college dorms, cars, and company offices across the globe. It's foolish to deceive ourselves into believing that it's okay to degrade our bodies and lend them out to random people in our lives.

I often aspire to access technology that could help me construct a time machine. I yearn to erase the hundreds of souls I've shared sexually within my lifetime. I wish I could go back and make certain that my wife would be my one and only sex partner. Then again, I understand that God is using my life as a testimony to help others overcome.

I pray regularly for God to give me words and actions to help ensure that my children understand how special they are. More importantly, I want them to grasp how significant they are to God. I want them to understand how awesome it is to be God's creation, pure and untouched. It hurts me to know that I didn't realize or understand how special I was growing up. I didn't know what it meant to be God's creation. I was very misguided. I guarded my money closer than my own flesh. I gave myself freely to anyone who looked appealing.

It devastates me, knowing that my wife may potentially cross paths with women I've been intimate with. I now understand the reason God asks us to remain pure until marriage. But we must remember, God is the ultimate mechanic. He can fix any part of us that is broken. He's that powerful! He won't change the past and there will be consequences for our sin—many of them we will have to deal with for long periods of time. But God has frequently shown me His ability to make miracles. Whatever mess we put ourselves into, He can pull us out of.

"Therefore do not let sin reign in your mortal body so that you obey its evil desires. Do not offer any part of yourself to sin as an instrument of wickedness, but rather offer yourselves to God as those who have been brought from death to life; and offer every part of yourself to him as an instrument of righteousness. For sin shall no longer be your master, because you are not under the law, but under grace."

—*Romans 6:12-14 (NIV)*

God's power and mercy gives us the authority to say No. No to porn and all moral filth. We can turn porn from a billion dollar industry to a nonexistent one. Be real with yourself today about porn and sexual immoral behavior. Remember the potential pregnancy scares, STDs, and lack of fulfillment. Contemplate the shame of knowing someone unworthy has a piece of you forever. Understand that our own willpower is not enough. Confess to God and surround yourself with others who will hold you accountable. It's time to get serious about sin and recognize when it causes us to stumble. *"And if your eye causes you to stumble, gouge it out and throw it away."(Matthew 18:9 NIV)*

It's time to leave a legacy of righteousness so that we may save our world and ourselves. Make the choice today to tear down the sin in your life. Do not stand for it any longer. Stand convicted and committed to change. Sin is a liar, but God is the truth.

11

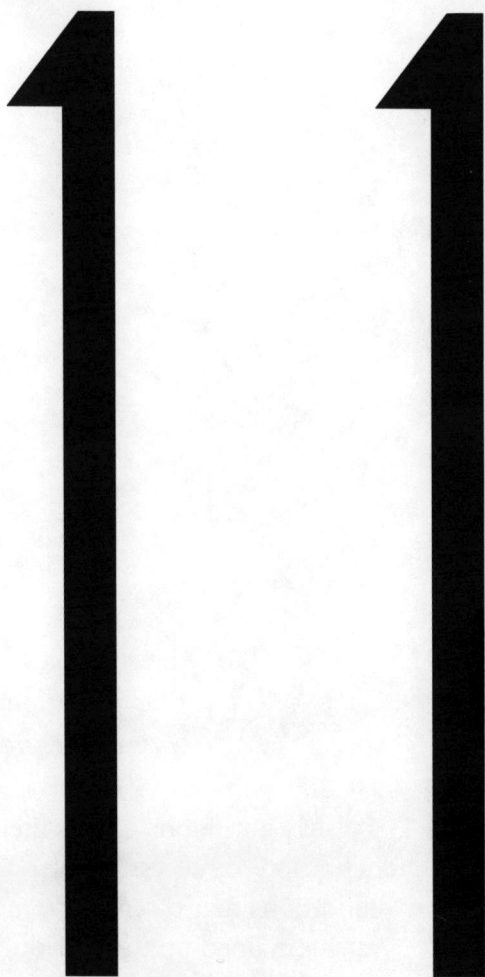

What Is Success?

What is success? When I looked up the definition, I found this: *The fact of getting or achieving wealth, respect, or fame.*

My entire pre-Christ life, I sold out to this definition of success. I toiled in environments and conditions that often made me feel inadequate— yet I remained on the worldly path that promised successful endings. Many of us are willing to sacrifice countless things to chase this definition of success. *(1 Timothy 6:4-10 NIV)* We give up relationships, material items, time, and often our beliefs. Nonetheless, God asks us to sacrifice these same things, yet we are often reluctant to do so.

I would like to think true success for all Christians would be eternal life in heaven? I finally realized that no matter what I accomplish on earth, my true success lies in my salvation. *Mark 8:36 (NIV)*, basically asks, what's the point of achieving worldly success, only to die and go to hell?

> **" Not everyone who says to me, Lord, Lord, will enter the kingdom of heaven, but only the one who does the will of my Father who is in heaven. Many will say to me on that day, Lord, Lord, did we not prophesy in your name and in your name drive out demons and in your name perform many miracles? Then I will tell them plainly, I never knew you. Away from me, you evildoers!"**

> *— Matthew 7:21-23*

How many of us are yearning for our moment to be called to hell? Would we truly enjoy the moment God tells us He never knew us? Heaven or hell seems to be the literal end all, be all, for all of us. The question we must ask ourselves is this: Are we striving daily to follow God's keys to salvation? One has taught me numerous steps on how to achieve success in Christ. Below are some vital keys to achieving true success (salvation)

Humility— It's the full understanding that *"I am a sinner."* An inability to acknowledge this makes me a liar, and Christ is not in me *(1 John 1:8 NIV)*. I have to realize that I can never be humble enough. My life has to become dedicated to growing more humble and less prideful on a daily basis. Without humility I cannot see the sin in my own life, making me non-relatable and ill-equipped to radically serve others. A lack of humility will ultimately stunt my potential for growth in Christ *(Matthew 7:3-5 NIV)* If given the choice, always take the low position, *"For all those who exalt themselves will be humbled, and those who humble themselves will be exalted." (Luke 18:9-14; Luke 14: 8-11 NIV)*

More God Less Me— God is not interested in watching me entertain my old life. Struggling with old friends and habits of the past is counterproductive. *(Matthew 10:37-42)* Often I've said to myself, *"I can't just change overnight,"*—what I'm really saying is, *"God I have major doubt in your power."* Jesus calls for a radical amputation. For my old life is what kept me away from His kingdom. Delighting in the sinful nature of my old self, only gets me closer to hell not Him. The day I was baptized into Christ, was the same day I decided to let Kellen die, become a new creation, and submerge myself in Jesus.

Giving— God has given us an abundance of resources here on earth. It is our job to share these, avoiding greed and giving abundantly to others. There is no reason anyone on earth should go without. Jesus was not concerned with storing up treasures on earth, He prefers that we store up treasures in heaven—our ultimate destination of success. God also gave His word, a blueprint to save us from our sin. It's imperative to share this gift with the world. It's the only way to save it. So give until it hurts, for Jesus gave His life so that we may live forever.

Love— Check out *1 Corinthians 13:4-7 (NIV)*. Anywhere that you read the word *love* insert your name instead. After reading this passage, ask yourself, *"Is this true?"* Am I patient? Am I kind? Do I keep no record of wrongs? If not, it's time to start loving. Loving others as God loves us will totally change our world.

Prayer— A successful step toward salvation is prayer. Early in my life with Christ I placed little importance on prayer. I couldn't see clearly the power in it. I personally define prayer as, *"anytime I speak to God."* It doesn't have to be something formal, at church, or before dinner *(although those are great places to do it)*. We can talk to God anywhere.

Prayer gets you closer to God, plain and simple. It creates an intimate relationship with Him that's indispensable. God yearns for us to talk to Him, He wants us to lay all of our worries onto His shoulders. Constantly I ask God to help me through rough times. Because I believe He peacefully removes sinful things from my heart. Frequently I am successful through Him.

Prayer promptly creates closeness with others. As I started to pray regularly, I often thought only of myself. I was too consumed with my own needs and desires. I now pray for hours, asking God to help people everywhere. Praying for others helps us draw closer to whomever we pray for. It's a caring habit and responsibility for all Christians. Imagine a world of people praying to a God that answers prayers. Visualize how cohesive we could be.

Give It All Away— *Matthew 13:44 (NIV) "The Kingdom of Heaven is like a treasure hidden in a field. When a man found it, he hid it again, and then in his joy went and sold all he had and brought that field."*
Sell all of your possessions! Get rid of the items in your life that are causing more harm than good: sin, baggage, and drama. Liberate yourself altogether. In addition, I have the perfect place for you to make an exchange—God's Pawn Shop—where trash and filth are made glorious! God's shop hands us treasures worth much more than the junk we turn over to Him. Find Heaven by getting rid of your hell.

Faith— *Matthew 17:20 (NIV) "Truly I tell you, if you have faith as small as a mustard seed, you can say to this mountain, move from here to there, and it will move. Nothing will be impossible for you."*
One has aided me with having higher levels of faith. I've witnessed many things change in my life using faith much smaller than a mustard seed. Faith is imperative in our walk with Christ. If I don't believe in Him wholeheartedly I compromise my successes through Him. Jesus is Lord! I believe

that with all my heart. I don't have time to doubt Him any longer. Have faith in God while remaining faithful to Him. Know and believe that through His word, His promises will ring true. *Hebrews 10: 35-36 (NIV)* " *So do not throw away your confidence; it will be richly rewarded. You need to persevere so that when you have done the will of God, you will receive what he has promised.* "

Forgiveness— Becoming a disciple of Christ helped me realize how many people I'd yet to forgive in my life. There was so much anger and hatred buried inside of me. An unforgiving heart builds a wall between God and us. It dims our light, hindering our ability to be an example of Christ. Because of God's love we are able to access His Heavenly promises. Forgiveness is our ticket to salvation. Who are we to keep grudges against anyone? We all sin and still God forgives. So we must to do the same.

Love Your Enemies— This may be the most difficult task in my walk—to love those who do not love me back. Fortunately, God provided a direct opportunity for me to practice what I preach and apply this word to my life. I struggle often with loving the mother of my first child. Frequently I feel she is selfish, dishonest, spiteful, and overall unloving. Many times I want to indulge in my selfish desires and showcase rage and pride to demand my respect. Wrongfully I believed that turning my cheek to her hurtful behavior got me nowhere. Only through His teachings have I been able to break down barriers between the two of us. God has taught me through numerous trial and error, *(the error is usually in my heart)* my desire to please myself and not Him, ultimately destroys communication with my daughter's mother. My sin of selfishness has never helped in the construction of a positive relationship with her. My prideful approach only damages whatever rapport we've built.

At some point someone has to take the Jesus route. Through humility, I am able to first see my errors, and they occur more often than I'd like to admit. Once realized, I am able to turn my cheek so that she may hit the other. God's law has allowed for our relationship to grow more positive for sure. Our communication is better, I've been taken off of child support, and we've lessened the ability for our child to manipulate us. Who was once my enemy *(my daughters mother)* is now my friend. For God's word says,

"Woe to you when everyone speaks well of you, for that is how their ancestors treated the false prophets. But to you who are listening I say: Love your enemies, do good to those who hate you, bless those who curse you, pray for those who mistreat you. If someone slaps you on one cheek, turn to them the other also. If someone takes your coat, do not withhold your shirt from them. Give to everyone who asks you, and if anyone takes what belongs to you, do not demand it back. Do to others as you would have them do to you. If you love those who

love you, what credit is that to you? Even sinners love those who love them. And if you do good to those who are good to you, what credit is that to you? Even sinners do that. And if you lend to those from whom you expect repayment, what credit is that to you? Even sinners lend to sinners, expecting to be repaid in full. But love your enemies, do good to them, and lend to them without expecting to get anything back. Then your reward will be great, and you will be children of the Most High, because he is kind to the ungrateful and wicked. Be merciful, just as your Father is merciful.

—Luke 6:26-36

Making Disciples— *Matthew 28:19 "Therefore go and make disciples of all nations baptizing them in the name of the Father and of the Son and of the Holy Spirit."* No matter what our age, race, gender, or financial status, Jesus calls us to make disciples! For the duration of His ministry, Jesus spent his time teaching twelve men. His dedication to His Father's Word, made it possible for us to see the light of God thousands of years later. In order to move this mission forward, we must be dedicated, genuine, and self-sacrificial—sharing our faith with the lost as often as possible—learning our Word, so that we can teach the goodness of God to all. God chose you so that you may have success in Him, the only success we need.

Be Bold—Lastly, we must be good sons and daughters of God in order to inherit the kingdom. Respect God like His children, not His slaves or servants. Take control of your life and have church everyday; in your homes, at work, and in your cars—pray with your families, friends, neighbors, and co-workers. When we begin to take this walk seriously, making God the number one priority of our lives, this world will become an incredible place. Remember, not all will follow, for the road to God is narrow and few find it. Nevertheless, together we can radically influence this world through our minds, bodies, and souls, making our planet a holy place dedicated to showcasing God's love to all who live. **Amen**

About The Author

*Kellen E. Brandon is a dedicated disciple
and entrepreneur serving God through his
publishing company (Brandon Publishing).
Born and raised in Flint, MI, one of
the most dangerous cities in the world,
Brandon undersands the urgency for
Christ in his community. Kellen resides in
Lansing, Michingan with his wfie and two
daughters.*

OneRelationship01@gmail.com

If you're looking to find strong relationships in Christ.

Email us at the address above.

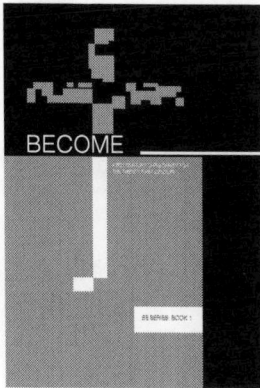

BECOME

By Joel Nagel

How Would Jesus make disciples?

He spoke to the crowds and did great miracles but he discipled only twelve. Remarkably, God's plan to save the world hinged on Jesus pouring Himself into just a few men. If this was the method that Jesus chose for the creation of the church, then we would be wise to imitate.

The Become Study Series puts the gospel message of Jesus Christ into the hands of His disciples. The topics, scriptures, and questions have been chosen to bring about incredible life change for the student as well as the teacher.

Order you copy of Become today on Amazon.com

Made in the USA
Charleston, SC
08 May 2014